BUSINESS THE

RICHARD
BRANSON
WAY

BIGSHOTS

BUSINESS THE

RICHARD

BRANSON

WAY

10 SECRETS OF THE WORLD'S GREATEST BRAND BUILDER

DES DEARLOVE

CAPSTONE

Copyright © Des Dearlove 1999, 2002

The right of Des Dearlove to be identified as the author of this work has been asserted in accordance with the Copyright, Designs and Patents Act 1988

First edition published 1999
Second edition published 2002
Capstone Publishing Limited (a Wiley company)
The Atrium
Southern Gate
Chichester
PO19 8SQ
www.wileyeurope.com
e-mail (for orders and customer service enquires): cs-books@wiley.co.uk

Reprinted May 2005

CIP catalogue records for this book are available from the British Library and the US Library of Congress

ISBN 10: 1-84112-149-5 (PB)   ISBN 13: 978-1-84112-149-9 (PB)

Typeset in 11/15 New Baskerville by
Sparks Computer Solutions Ltd, Oxford
http://www.sparks.co.uk
Printed and bound by
T.J. International Ltd, Padstow, Cornwall

This book is printed on acid-free paper

Substantial discounts on bulk quantities of Capstone books are available to corporations, professional associations and other organizations. Please contact John Wiley & Sons for more details on 212 850 6000 or (fax) 212 850 6088 or (e-mail) info@wiley-capstone.co.uk

Business The Richard Branson Way was written independently by the author, Des Dearlove. It has not been authorized by its subject.

CONTENTS

ACKNOWLEDGMENTS

I'd like to think this book provides a fair analysis of why Richard Branson has been so successful over so many years. In the end, though, whether you see him as the bearded crusader or simply capitalism with a hairy face, it is impossible to escape the conclusion that he is a remarkable individual. For three decades he has dazzled the British business scene with a unique mixture of substance and style. At the very least, he has brought colour and fun into the otherwise all too grey lives of countless business journalists around the world. Richard, for that you have my heartfelt thanks.

In researching this book, I have plundered a veritable treasure trove of articles, as well as two excellent biographies. I would particularly like to thank Mick Brown and Tim Jackson, whose books were an inspiration; Alan Mitchell of Amrop International; and a cast of thousands who have interviewed and analysed Branson over the years.

I would also like to thank: Stephen Coomber for his research and insights; and Mark Allin, Richard Burton and Catherine Meyrick at Capstone Publishing for their patience. (We got there in the end). Finally, I'd like to thank Stuart Crainer for such a splendid day out on the river.

Des Dearlove
August 1998

RICHARD BRANSON REVISITED ...

A lot has happened to Richard Branson since the first edition of this book was written. Not all of it has gone his way. Indeed, Branson has suffered his share of setbacks – which makes this second edition all the more timely. Some commentators have suggested that Branson may have lost his Midas touch. But this seems premature. Rather, the roller-coaster ride that has characterized his career continues apace. One of Branson's enduring strengths is his ability to absorb punches, to take the rough with the smooth. Branson has bounced back many times. Recent months have brought new challenges for the great entrepreneurial adventurer.

In 1999, the year after *Business The Richard Branson Way* was first published, Branson featured in *Forbes* magazine's list of the World's Richest People with a fortune estimated at $2.6 billion. By 2000 that figure had risen to $3.3 billion. Yet in 2001, Branson's net worth had declined to some $1.8 billion. Part of the reason for this sharp reduction in value was plainly outside of Branson's influence; a global economic slowdown. Yet he had also suffered some very public and potentially avoidable setbacks. So what has happened to temporarily wipe that characteristically toothy grin off the face of the UK's most avuncular tycoon?

For a start, there was Branson's unrequited ambition to host the UK's National Lottery. After his first abortive attempt to bid for the National Lottery franchise in 1994, Branson might have been expected to tear up his ticket. It was clear from the accusations and recriminations in the wake of the decision by the National Lottery Commission to award the franchise to the rival bidder, Camelot, that Branson was aggrieved. But he is not a man to be easily shaken from his purpose. Instead of giving up on his ambition to run "The People's Lottery," he waited for the next round. Characteristically, for a man who likes to challenge the status quo, Branson was back in line for the franchise when it came up again in 2001.

This time around Branson had good reason to think he would succeed. The momentum seemed to be with him. He launched his bid with the customary Branson razzmatazz – a jazz band, actors in nurses' and firemen's costumes, and enormous inflatable lottery balls. His chances looked better than good. The Lottery Commission gave out good vibes. Branson had partnered with some powerful allies. He had the technology. Included in his consortium applying for the seven-year license to run the lottery were the software giant Microsoft, and network company Cisco. Branson promised to create "a millionaire a day" by introducing new improved games and increasing participation. Crucially, The People's Lottery would, he claimed, return more funds to charity than the incumbent operator Camelot. But Branson didn't get the chance to prove his claims.

In truth the process to award the new license for the National Lottery was shambolic. Branson announced his intention to challenge Camelot in December 1999. His bid was submitted by the deadline for February 2000, and after being asked to substantially improve the bid, it was resubmitted by mid-July.

The announcement of the winner of the two-horse race between Camelot and The People's Lottery was set for August 2000. But then, in a confusing decision, both bids were rejected. More confusion ensued when the lottery commission decided to go forward with one of the bids only – The People's Lottery. It looked like game over, Branson wins. But it proved otherwise. Camelot challenged the Lottery Commission's decision in the High Court – and won. Dame Helena Shovelton, chair of the commission resigned, and both bidders resubmitted their bids. The winner was announced in December 2000 – it wasn't Branson.

The whole process was a fiasco and Branson was, understandably, furious. At first there were mutterings of a legal challenge to the decision. In the end Branson decided to walk away because, he said, of the potential damage to confidence in the lottery. He was, he said, "bitterly disappointed" at a decision that he considered "cowardly" and "substantively unfair." He also ruled out any future bid for the franchise. A subsequent claim for compensation by The People's Lottery for £18.5 million was rejected by the National Lottery Commission in April 2001.

As if that wasn't bad enough, Branson's reputation has also been dented by his foray into train services. Any notion that running a dilapidated train service would be like running an airline quickly vanished. Virgin Trains' services hit the buffers early on and never got back on track. The Virgin Trains railway franchises have plumbed new depths of train service misery. This is quite an achievement in the UK where trains are famously inefficient. It's tempting to feel sorry for Branson. The rail franchises have become something of a poisoned chalice. No matter what Branson says or does the bad publicity from Virgin's tardy railway operations just keeps coming.

In 1999, figures from the shadow strategic rail authority showed that Virgin Trains had the worst record for punctuality in the country. In February 2001, following the fatal Hatfield railway crash, Branson launched a half-price, rail-fare bonanza in an attempt to woo travelers back to the railways. He promised, "to capture the imagination of passengers who have suffered traffic jams." Unfortunately, the reality was people jams – with huge queues and long waits for tickets, whether buying tickets over the phone or in person. Virgin Trains had underestimated the demand. There were 376,000 calls on one Monday to Virgin's call center in Scotland, compared to 20,000 on an average day, and a 600 percent increase in enquiries to the booking office. The ensuing chaos and adverse publicity turned a genuine and generous offer into a potential PR disaster.

There was worse to come. The half-price ticket episode was followed by the " nightmare" train journey; a 16-hour ordeal for passengers traveling from Newcastle to Plymouth. The train left at 3.00 p.m. on Monday afternoon and was scheduled to arrive in Plymouth at 10.25 p.m. Passengers finally reached their destination at 7.00 a.m. the following morning. The ill-fated train suffered numerous setbacks. Flooding caused the service to be replaced by coaches, and then one of the replacement coaches broke down on the motorway and was delayed for four hours while being repaired. One of the passengers said: "We were all handed meal vouchers at Birmingham, but I didn't hear an apology of any kind." In September 2001, passengers in the guise of the North-West Rail Passengers Committee were complaining that Virgin Trains had increased some fares by up to 80 percent over the previous three years.

This is all very strange for a company with the Virgin name. Virgin Trains appears to be the antithesis of everything Richard Branson stands for. Branson has always gone to great lengths to protect his brand image, knowing that maintaining public trust and confidence in the Virgin name underpins the success of the whole Virgin Group. The poor performance of Virgin Trains threatens to undermine that trust. In his defense, Virgin Trains inherited 30-year-old rolling stock, running on a railway that had been underfunded for years. And when Branson took up the challenge of running the rail franchises he acknowledged that it would take five years to turn the lines operated from the worst in the country to the best. But even Branson's well-hone PR skills have not been able to deflect the criticism. The planned introduction of tilting trains by 2003, traveling at speeds of up to 140 miles per hour drastically cutting journey times, as well as the replacement of all old rolling stock, could go some way to salvaging Virgin Trains' tarnished image.

Elsewhere in the Virgin empire, however, it has been business as usual. New Virgin ventures continue to be added to the eclectic collection of companies gathered under the umbrella of the seemingly infinitely elastic Virgin brand. Virgin Mobile was launched at the end of 1999 to sell mobile phones and provide mobile phone services. Other additions included Virgin Active, a health and fitness company, Virgin Cars, an online car retailer, and virgin.com, offering a raft of Virgin products over the Internet, to name but a few.

Meanwhile, Branson continues to meet with the occasional failure – much as he always has. Virgin Cola, for example, which had hoped to take the American cola market by storm, lost its fizz and retreated from the US market in 2000.

What began so promisingly ended in a salutary lesson for upstarts everywhere. Launching Virgin Cola in the US, Branson donned army fatigues and rode into Times Square in a battle tank to beat the drum for his assault on the cola market. The carefully choreographed show of bravado was emblazoned across American newspapers and TV screens. But in February 2000, Virgin admitted defeat in its war against Coca-Cola and Pepsi-Cola in the US. After making scarcely a dent in the cola market, Virgin was forced to change the strategy, management and location of its soft drinks business. It will now concentrate on "new age" drinks, including fruit juices and energy beverages.

Critics may argue that the failed cola expedition proves that there is a limit to how far a brand can be stretched. But the real lessons lie elsewhere. Branson has made a career out of playing David to the other guy's Goliath. His greatest weapon is guile. He delights in taking on, and outmaneuvering large corporations. So what went wrong in the cola skirmish? Virgin Cola grew out the development of a premium cola formula by a Canadian company called Cott. The company approached Branson with the proposition of putting the Virgin brand on the new formula. Branson's immediate concern was the level of comeback from Pepsi and Coca-Cola. In the UK, Virgin Cola was created in just eight weeks. There simply wasn't time for the big cola companies to put their defensive plans in place. In November 1994, Virgin Cola was launched and managed to seize a seven percent share of the take-home market.

But hubris set in when Virgin decided to take on the cola giants in a pitched battle. Efforts to launch Virgin Cola in Australia failed and market shares in France, Belgium and Japan remain miniscule. The decision to take the fight to the cola heartlands of the American domestic market was a show of bravado rather than business sense. Pitted against the might of the cola barons, Virgin failed because it ignored the basic rules of successful guerrilla warfare: it gave up the advantage of home territory; and it lost the vital element of surprise. Without these, Virgin was just another brand.

Branson is a business buccaneer. The cola escapade, however, should be a reminder that some treasure ships are more heavily armed than others. In a straight fight it was always going to be about firepower. Virgin was simply outgunned.

Yet, Branson's business career has never been all plain sailing. The ill-fated cola expedition is typical. Nothing ventured, nothing gained is how he views the marketplace. On balance, his successes greatly outweigh his failures. His occasional setbacks prompt periodic media rumblings that the Virgin empire is financially overextended. But closer inspection reveals that Branson continues to pursue a partnership strategy for a large proportion of his ventures. He rarely bears the whole risk of a business entirely on his own. Instead Virgin's usual practice is to take a majority interest in a new venture, with the partner taking the rest of the stock.

So, for example, Singapore Airlines holds 49 percent of Virgin Atlantic; Virgin Mobile is a joint venture with One 2 One; cable company NTL owns 49 percent of Virgin.net; and the financial position of the Virgin companies is constantly shifting as Branson extends or reduces his holdings. This places Branson in a better position to survive difficult trading conditions.

As Branson steers the Virgin group into the 21st century there is no reason to suspect that he will apply any more restraint towards expanding the Virgin brand that he has in the past. And, while the years following the publication of the first edition of this book have provided some difficult challenges for the consumers' champion there have been a few notable causes for celebration.

On March 30th, 2000, plain Richard Branson became Sir Richard Branson. Knighted in the New Year's Honours List for services to entrepreneurship, the habitually casually attired Branson donned a morning suit for the first time ever at his investiture ceremony at Buckingham Palace. Respectability beckoned. But so far he has stoutly resisted the temptation to join the establishment. With typical *élan*, party-loving Branson celebrated his knighthood by holding a reception for the 250 others receiving honours on the same day. When asked how it felt to be "Sir Richard," Branson answered: "It feels great. It feels odd sleeping with a Lady though."

THE LIFE AND TIMES OF RICHARD BRANSON

In the modern world of business, Richard Branson is an anomaly. In an era dominated by strategists, he is an opportunist. Through his company the Virgin Group, he has created a unique business phenomenon. Never before has a single brand been so successfully deployed across such a diverse range of goods and services. The distinctive red and white Virgin logo, it seems, is as elastic as Mates condoms – just one of the many products it promotes.[1] Branson is the ultimate brand-builder.

THE BRANSON PHENOMENON

In the film *Four Weddings and a Funeral*, a character jokes that his friend must be the richest man in Britain, but the friend says: "Of course not. There's the queen. And that Branson bloke is doing terribly well."

Britain's best known entrepreneur, Branson has been doing "terribly well" for more than three decades now. He started his first business at the age of 16, and was a millionaire at 24. Now in his 50s, Branson is a regular entry in *Forbes* magazine's list of the richest men in the world.

His personal wealth has been estimated at $1.8 billion, but it's hard to get an accurate tally, since his companies are private, constantly dividing and multiplying, and are controlled via a series of tax-efficient offshore trusts – all perfectly legal and above board, but hard to untangle.

Today, Branson is the driving force at the centre of a web of more than 200 companies, employing more than 25,000 people in 26 countries. His commercial interests span travel, hotels, consumer goods, computer games, music and airlines. You can even buy a Virgin pension or investment plan.

But financial services is a far cry from the adolescent record label that helped put Punk on the map in the 1980s, with a controversially named album by the Sex Pistols. Everything about the record suggested rebellion – including the Pistol's rendition of "God Save the Queen"; but the album was a stepping stone for Branson.

By then, Virgin had already won the respect of the hippy generation with *Tubular Bells*, from a young unknown artist called Mike Oldfield. *Never Mind the Bollocks* was the perfect product to establish the Virgin brand with a new generation of spiky-haired teenagers. Branson had created a new fusion of rebellion and business – and discovered a unique new brand proposition. He has been repeating the formula ever since.

Yet Branson is more than just a businessman, he is a popular public figure – admired by parents and young people alike. One of a generation of business leaders who grew up in the 1960s, he has been described as a "hippy capitalist." To this, he has added a reputation as an adventurer – setting a new world record for crossing the Atlantic, and almost losing his life trying to circumnavigate the globe in a hot air balloon.

His derring-do outside of business life is matched by the boldness of his escapades in it. He has repeatedly used the Virgin brand to take on aggressive market leaders and shake up complacent markets – first the big record companies, then the airlines and more recently soft drinks and financial services. These commercial adventures have almost bankrupted the company on several occasions. They have earned him a special place in the affections of first the British public and now the world.

> "A ruthlessly ambitious workaholic."

But his popular image belies another side to Branson.[2] Despite his wealth, he remains unrelenting in his commercial ambitions. At times, he seems to launch new ventures on an almost daily basis. "A ruthlessly ambitious workaholic," is how one biographer described him.

Branson claims that Virgin was started from a public phone booth with less capital than most people would happily "blow" on a good night out at a restaurant. Anecdote and myth surrounds him. Yet Branson the businessman and master brand-builder remains shrouded in a public relations smoke screen.

THE UNIVERSAL BRAND

Branson's greatest commercial achievement, to date, is to create what is arguably the world's first universal brand. Other famous names have become synonymous with the product they adorn: Hoover vacuum cleaners, Coca-Cola, and Levi Strauss to name just a few. But only Virgin transcends products.

Yet despite its remarkable success, Branson would have us believe that none of it was planned. He gives the impression that the Virgin phenomenon is one of those odd things that happen to people sometimes. This is part of the Branson mystique. He makes it look and sound so simple.

> **"It would have been interesting to have tracked the success of the Virgin companies or otherwise if we had called the company Slipped Disc Records. Slipped Disc Condoms might not have worked as well."**

"When we came up with the name 'Virgin' instead of 'Slipped Disc' Records for our record company in the winter of 1969, I had some vague idea of the name being catchy and applying to lots of other products for young people."[3]

"It would have been interesting to have tracked the success of the Virgin companies or otherwise if we had called the company Slipped Disc Records. Slipped Disc Condoms might not have worked as well."

The quip is typical of a man who has lived his whole life like some big adventure. An outspoken critic of business schools and management theory, Branson likes to portray himself as the ordinary man on the street (despite his comfortable middle class origins). He is the small guy who outsmarts the big guys. His account of how the famous Virgin logo came to be is typical of the way things seem to happen at Virgin.

"When Virgin Records became successful we followed our instincts …," Branson explains. "Initially the music reflected the 'hippy' era and our logo of a naked lady back to back reflected that too. Then when Punk came along we felt we needed a crisper image … Rather than spending a fortune coming up with the new image, I was talking to our graphic designer one day explaining what we wanted and he threw on the floor his doodling – the now famous Virgin signature – which I fortunately picked up on the way to the loo."

It sounds so casual, but the words mask an extraordinary entrepreneurial mind, one that has reinvented business to fit the times he lives in.

CORPORATE ROCK STAR

But Branson is more than just a successful businessman. He is one of a new breed of entrepreneurs whose celebrity status and irreverent approach means they have more in common with rock stars than the "suits" who populate the business world.

Along with Anita Roddick, Ben & Jerry of ice cream fame, Bill Gates and Ted Turner, Branson has become a cultural icon. Part of a new generation of business leaders, his alternative business philosophy is a vital part of the Virgin brand appeal.

No one plays the David to the Goliath of "Big Business" better than Richard Branson.

Branson deliberately targets markets where the customer has been consistently ripped-off or under-served, and the competition is complacent. He delights in casting Virgin as the cheeky underdog, faster on its feet and nipping at the heels of big business. No one plays the David to the Goliath of "Big Business" better than Richard Branson. It is a marketing strategy that appeals to millions.

Wherever it appears, the Virgin logo attracts its own anti-establishment consumers. Branson himself – with his long hair, toothy grin and outrageous behavior – is as famous as the company. If anything, he is better known than many of the rock stars he helped create. (In business school-speak, Branson personally accounts for a major chunk of the company's intellectual capital.)

Love him or hate him, Branson is one of the most successful businessmen on the planet. But his influence and popularity extend far beyond the business world. Among business tycoons, he and Ted Turner stand out as adventurers as well as successful entrepreneurs. Branson's forays into the record books include the fastest crossing of the Atlantic by sea in Virgin Atlantic Challenger; and several attempts to circumnavigate the globe in a hot-air balloon.

Along the way, too, Branson has managed to endear himself to the British public in a way that no other entrepreneur ever has. He fought to make the National Lottery a non-profitmaking venture with the proceeds going to worthy causes; he headed up a government environmental campaign; and launched Mates condoms to raise awareness about AIDS. His face appears on the front pages of the national press and television almost as often as the Royal Family.

Yet, despite being a billionaire with his own Caribbean Island to retreat to, Branson has somehow retained the common touch. Unlike other celebrities in the public eye he has also managed to protect his privacy. We only see Branson when he wants us to. He is almost as adept at avoiding bad publicity as he is at creating positive coverage.

He has also managed to keep a veil around the inner workings of his financial empire. In 1986 he floated his Virgin business on the London Stock Exchange, only to buy it back because he didn't like the constraints a market listing brought with it. (The 1987 Stock Market crash wiped £millions off the value of the company overnight, confirming his distrust of the suits from the investment communities of Wall Street and the City of London, and goading him into taking back control.)

Taking the company back into private ownership has allowed Branson to shield its innermost workings from the public gaze. It has enabled him to create a business empire that is very different to the norm. Instead of the traditional model of a handful of operating companies reporting to a holding company, Virgin is an atomized empire – a myriad of businesses loosely bound together by the Virgin brand, many of them joint ventures with outside investors: a network that seems to have little in common except the name. Only Richard Branson and a handful of his senior executives have an overall view. Most of them are virtually unknown to the public. The group's chairman and founder, however, is an integral part of the Virgin brand.

Here, too, there is paradox. The public Branson is instantly recognizable to millions of people. His is the affable and caring face of business. The man who has made a career out of taking on big business and winning; the man who prefers brightly colored sweaters to the conventional corporate suit and tie. But the private Branson is much less well known.

Indeed, it has been suggested that there are two Richard Bransons: the people's champion known to millions and the deal maker known only to his business partners.

According to Tim Jackson, author of "Virgin King" the unofficial Branson biography, Branson's motto should be *ars est celare artem* – the art lies in concealing the art. This is the essence of the Branson management style, and the cornerstone of the Virgin empire.

THE EARLY YEARS

Richard Charles Nicholas Branson was born on 18 July 1950. By the time baby Richard arrived, his father Edward Branson and mother Eve Branson had settled in the sleepy village of Shamley Green in the Surrey stockbroker belt. With Ted Branson only recently qualified as a barrister, money was tight and the family rented a rambling and somewhat ramshackle house for 12 shillings a week.

His formal education was conventional, and started at Scaitcliffe Preparatory School. The young Branson was not academically minded and only scraped into public school at Stowe after a spell at a crammer.

Although he liked sport, the finer points of a classical British education were wasted on him, but the experience was invaluable for his future career. Traditional in every sense of the word, the school provided the perfect education for the well-spoken young man who would go on to build a business empire that traded on bucking the system.

In those early years glimpses of the Branson psychology are already evident.

As one commentator observed: "The fresh-faced young lad had only scraped in to his minor public school after special tutoring for the entry exam. Subsequently he had failed his elementary mathematics three times. Yet still he was in no doubt that he could do a better job of running the school than the powers that be. So he penned the headmaster a memo, outlining his suggestions. Among them: allow sixth formers to drink two pints of beer a day."

But Branson never made it into the sixth form. He dropped out of school at 16, his head too full of big ideas and business schemes to take in anything else. At the time, his headmaster observed that Branson would end up either a millionaire or behind bars. The rest, as they say, is history (although in the event it was a close call between the two).

A quarter of a century later, Branson is known the world over. The exuberant business buccaneer who flew in the face of received wisdom in the airline industry and turned up the volume on the big record labels, who shook up the cola giants, and gave the UK financial services firms a good run for their money; the adventurer who broke the trans-Atlantic speed record; the daredevil hot air balloonist. Above all he is known as the David who took on Goliath in the shape of British Airways, dirty tricks and all – and won. But it could have been very different.

TYCOON-IN-WAITING

Branson's first business ventures began at school. With Nick Powell, his childhood friend and long-time business partner, the young Branson cut his business teeth first breeding budgerigars, and then growing Christmas trees. Both failed.

His first proper business – a magazine called *Student*, was launched when he was just 16 years old – and was not a resounding success either. Then, something happened (and has kept on happening ever since). With little or no knowledge of pop music, Branson stumbled onto the idea of a mail order record company. Short of advertisements, he published his own ad in the magazine.

The year was 1969, and London was ripe for mail order music. The first the young entrepreneur knew of it was when checks started arriving through the letter box. The business took off. Richard Branson was airborne.

Serendipity, too, played its part in his move from mail order to record stores; a postal strike crippled the mail order business, forcing him to seek new outlets. He opened his first store in Oxford Street in 1971.

An early skirmish with HM Customs & Excise taught Branson the sense of staying on the right side of the law – and the value of good legal and financial advisers, something which has stood him in good stead ever since. The young entrepreneur had discovered a loophole in the tax system. Records that were for export did not incur tax. But the customs officials didn't check which albums were being shipped. It was just too tempting to send worthless old stock to Europe and sell the new stock in the UK without paying any tax on them. When the scam was uncovered, Branson was arrested and threatened with prosecution – a threat only withdrawn when he agreed to pay back the money he owed.

From his Virgin record shops Branson moved into record production, launching a highly successful record label. One of the first artists it signed was Mike Oldfield, whose album *Tubular Bells* stayed in the UK charts for the next ten years. The proceeds from *Tubular Bells* bankrolled the Virgin empire.

In the 1980s, the Virgin label became synonymous with a string of radical young musicians. It helped put Punk on the map with a young band called the Sex Pistols. In 1982, Virgin discovered Boy George and Culture Club. The cash generated by the Virgin record label meant that Branson could begin building his empire in earnest.

By 1984 Virgin was literally airborne. Branson had migrated from pop music to transatlantic flight, launching Virgin Atlantic Airways. A year later, Virgin minus the airline, which Branson retained, was floated on the London Stock Market. But the crash of 1987 and his general misgivings about the financial community convinced Branson to take the extraordinary step of taking the company back into private ownership.

The rest, as they say, is history. Today, the Virgin empire spans air travel, holidays, clothing, record stores, soft drinks, radio … the list goes on and on. But how did Richard Branson shrug off some of the fiercest competitors in Britain and America to create the most powerful brand in the world? And what are the lessons for the entrepreneurs of tomorrow?

BUSINESS STRATEGY

Branson has probably never heard of Michael Porter's five forces – even though the Harvard Business School professor has been essential reading for business school graduates for more than 20 years. If he had, he would know that the airline business, the cola market and the UK financial services markets – to name just some of the areas where he has successfully set up Virgin companies – are textbook examples of extreme competitiveness or high barriers to entry, and best avoided. (Asked how one becomes a millionaire, Branson replies that you start off as a billionaire and then open an airline.) That might have deprived us of one of the most colorful and dynamic business empires the world has ever seen.

> Asked how one becomes a millionaire, Branson replies that you start off as a billionaire and then open an airline.

On the other hand, Branson's reaction to being told something is impossible is usually to regard it as a challenge. Porter's analysis would probably have inspired him. It is precisely because Branson doesn't read the business text books that he is so successful. (Many of the techniques he introduced in the 1960s are now being held up as panaceas for management in the 21st Century.)

CORE COMPETENCIES

In an uncharacteristic reference to business school theory, the ideas of Gary Hamel and C.K. Prahalad in particular, in recent years Branson has distilled Virgin's four core competencies. These are:

◆ The ability to identify appropriate growth opportunities

◆ The ability to move quickly

◆ The willingness to give day-to-day management control to relatively small operating teams. "We try to keep our companies small," he says. (Even though the airline now has 6000 staff, Branson likes to think it has "retained a small company environment and informality.")

◆ The ability to create and manage effective joint ventures.

Others have suggested Branson's own real core competence is the ability to motivate people and push them to the limit. Still others, point to his relentless and sometimes ruthless negotiating skills.

Careful dissection, however, reveals that the truth is more subtle. The Branson phenomenon can be reduced to a number of lessons that can sharpen the business acumen of any manager or entrepreneur. But that doesn't mean that the formula can be duplicated. What the analysis shows is that it takes a very special individual to run a business the Branson way. The question is, do you have what it takes to be a Richard Branson?

BRANSON'S WORLD

A brief history of Virgin:

1950 Richard Charles Nicholas Branson born, first child of Edward Branson, barrister, and Eve Branson, former dancer and air stewardess.

1964 Admitted to Stowe School, Buckinghamshire.

1966 Branson founds *Student* magazine with a school friend.

1967 Branson leaves school after O levels and moves to London to concentrate on magazine.

1968 January 26, first issue of *Student Magazine*, Richard Branson's first business venture is produced. Branson founds non-profit Student Advisory Centre.

1969 Branson takes out High Court writ to force the Beatles to provide recording for *Student's* front cover. First advertisement for mail order record business appears in last issue of *Student*.

1970 Start of Virgin mail-order operation. Branson fined £7 for using words "venereal disease" in publicity material for Student Advisory Centre.

1971 Postal strike. First Virgin record store opens in London's Oxford Street. Simon Draper, Branson's South African cousin, joins Virgin. Raided by HM Customs & Excise, the UK tax authorities; Branson arrested for purchase tax fraud. Agrees to pay £53,000 in tax and duties over next three years. Prosecution is dropped.

1972 First Virgin recording studio opens at "The Manor" near Oxford, England. Mike Oldfield starts recording *Tubular Bells*. Branson marries first wife Kristen Tomassi.

1973 Virgin Record label is launched with *Tubular Bells* becoming one of the biggest selling records of the decade. Music publishing business established in the UK.

1975 Branson unsuccessfully tries to sign the Rolling Stones and 10CC.

1976 Sex Pistols cause furore when they swear on early evening TV. TV presenter Bill Grundy is fired.

1977 Virgin signs the Sex Pistols after both EMI and A&M have decided they are too controversial.

1978 The Venue, Virgin's first night club, opens ... Human League signed to Virgin record label.

1980 Virgin Records moves into overseas markets, initially through licensing deals but later through its own subsidiaries in France and then elsewhere.

1981 Phil Collins signs to Virgin.

1982 Virgin talent scout discovers Boy George. Culture Club signs to Virgin for worldwide rights.

1983 Virgin Vision (forerunner of Virgin Communications) is formed to distribute films and videos. Vanson Developments, Virgin's property company is formed. Virgin Games (computer games software publisher) is launched ... Virgin Group's combined pre-tax profit rises to £2 million on turnover of just under £50 million.

1984 Virgin Atlantic Airways and Virgin Cargo are launched. Acquisition of interest in luxury hotel in Deya, Mallorca, forerunner to hotel operations in UK and Caribbean. Don Cruickshank hired as Virgin's new group managing director; Trevor Abbott brought in as finance director. Virgin Vision launches "The Music Channel," a 24-hour satellite-delivered music station and produces the award-winning film *1984*.

1985 £25 million placing of 7% Convertible Stock is completed with 25 English and Scottish institutions, in the run up to floating the company. Branson transfers bulk of Virgin shareholding to offshore trusts

Virgin wins a Business Enterprise Award for company of the year. Virgin Holidays is formed. Branson joins unsuccessful Challenger attempt on Atlantic crossing record.

1986   Virgin Group, comprising the music, retail and property, and communications divisions, is floated on the London Stock Exchange. (Airline, clubs, holidays and aviation services remain part of privately owned company called Voyager Group.) Branson breaks Atlantic sea speed record in Challenger II, winning huge publicity.

1987   Virgin Records America is launched, quickly followed by subsidiary in Japan. BSB.Virgin sets up 525 post production facility in Los Angeles to work on high quality commercials and pop videos. Stock market crashes, Virgin share price falls back to below 90p. Branson forced to abandon attempt at hostile takeover of EMI. Mates condoms launched, with proceeds to go to Healthcare Foundation. Virgin directors veto use of company name on condom venture. Virgin shares listed on NASDAQ exchange in US.

1988   Richard Branson announces management buy-out of Virgin Group, following the stock market crash in October. Branson and other Virgin directors buy company from other shareholders with loan of £182.5 million.

1989   Virgin Atlantic Airways announces doubled pre-tax profits at £10 million. Cruickshank resigns as Group MD, Abbott takes over. Branson marries Joan Templeman.

1990   Branson and Per Lindstrand fly Pacific in hot air balloon. Gulf War breaks out during flight triggering airline recession. Virgin Atlantic sends 747 to Iraq to pick up British hostages. Virgin Retail Group and Marui (Japanese retailer) announce the formation of 50:50 joint venture company to operate Megastores in Japan.

1991   Virgin Publishing is formed by combining WH Allen, Allison & Busby and Virgin Books.
         Virgin operates first Heathrow services. Virgin sells 50 % of Megastores business to WHSmith. Branson decides to sell Virgin Music Group – "the jewel in the crown."

1992   Sale of Virgin Music Group to THORN EMI. The deal values Virgin Music Group at US $1 billion, with Richard Branson to remain non-executive president of the group. Post production interests are reorganized under a new holding company Virgin Television. US carrier Vintage Airtours is established to operate a daily service from Orlando to Florida Keys, offering nostalgic trips in DC–3. Branson threatens libel action against British Airways for dismissing his allegations of "dirty tricks" as publicity seeking.

1993   British Airways settles libel action for £610,000 plus all legal costs (total costs believed to exceed £4.5 million). Virgin Atlantic voted airline of the year by *Executive Travel* magazine for the third year running. Virgin Radio 1215 AM launched.

1994   Branson bids for franchise to run Britain's National Lottery, promising to give all profits to charitable foundation. Lottery awarded to rival Camelot consortium.

   Virgin Atlantic takes $325 million anti-trust case against British Airways to US court. Branson family narrowly escapes death in car crash on M40 motorway.

   Virgin Cola launched with much fanfare.

1995   Virgin Direct Personal Financial Service is launched. Virgin, TPG Partners, a major US investment fund and Hotel Properties Ltd announce the acquisition of MGM Cinemas. Australian Mutual Provincial (AMP) buys a 50% stake in Virgin Direct, buying out Norwich Union, the original partner.

1996   Virgin Bride, the largest bridal retail shop in Europe is launched in London. Virgin enters the Internet market with Virgin.net. Virgin Rail Group wins franchise to operate InterCity Express services linking 130 stations across Britain.

1997   Virgin's bid to operate the InterCity West Coast train service is successful, with a 15 year rail franchise. Virgin Vie, a new joint venture cosmetics and beauty care company, launches its four flagship stores in Britain. Virgin Direct launches its first banking product, Virgin One Account. Chris Evans' Ginger Productions acquires Virgin Radio for £85 million. The company, renamed Ginger Media Group, to be run by the existing staff under the Virgin Radio name.

1998 Virgin Trading purchases remaining stake in Virgin Cola from Cott Europe, taking full control of sales, marketing, logistics and distribution.

1999 Branson knighted in New Year's Honours List. Sells 49 percent of Virgin Atlantic to Singapore Airlines. Virgin Mobile launched.

2000 Loses second bid to operate the National Lottery, after a selection process dogged by controversy hands it to incumbent, Camelot. Virgin Clothing folds in the UK. Virgin Cars launched.

2001 Sells stake in mortgage brokerage Virgin One to Royal Bank of Scotland. Virgin Trains launches "world's biggest rail offer." Cuts almost all rail fares by 50 percent. Promotion doesn't run as smoothly as Virgin would like.

NOTES

1   Curiously enough, Virgin's executives originally refused to let Branson use the Virgin brand on contraceptives, fearing it would be too controversial.

2   Jackson, Tim, *Virgin King*, HarperCollins, London, 1994.

3   Branson, Richard, BBC 'Money Programme' Lecture, 1998.

One

PICK ON SOMEONE BIGGER THAN YOU

"At Virgin, we have a strategy of using the credibility of our brand to challenge the dominant players in a range of industries where we believe the consumer is not getting value for money."
– Richard Branson

Richard Branson has made a career out of playing David to the other guy's Goliath. In the past two decades, Virgin has crossed swords with some of the most powerful companies on the planet. In the 1970s, the Virgin record label went up against the music establishment, including the likes of EMI. When he set up Virgin Atlantic Airways in the 1980s, Branson took on the big airlines, going head to head with British Airways. In the 1990s, Virgin entered the soft drinks market with of all things a cola – placing it in direct competition with the giants of Coca-Cola and Pepsi Co. In financial services, Virgin Direct competes with the banks and other large-scale financial institutions.

Where some entrepreneurs might take one look at the market dominance of the big players and think better of it, Branson actually delights in taking on, and outmaneuvering large corporations. When Branson launched Virgin cola, one journalist noted: "I got the impression it was not the money but the prospect of taking on the mighty Coca-Cola corporation that really gave him his kicks."[1]

"Virgin stands for a sense of challenge," says Branson. "We like to use the brand to take on some very large companies, whom we believe exert too much power. There are cases where a brand name has traditionally been almost synonymous with the product it is selling – Coca-Cola, Kellogg's, Hoover for example – with heavy advertising to keep it that way. In fact, many American brand names like these grew up during the so-called era of the robber barons which led to the introduction of America's excellent anti-trust laws in the early 20th Century."

RICHARD THE LIONHEART

Branson has a remarkable ability to clothe almost everything he does in a crusading cloak. This lends the Virgin brand moral authority. When pitted against the immensely powerful forces of "big business," Branson-style capitalism looks almost saintly by comparison. By targeting companies with dominant and often aggressive market positions, Virgin is able to seize the moral high ground from the outset, something that gives it a distinctive edge with consumers.

Where other empire builders get involved in commercial dog-fights, Branson goes in for crusades – with Virgin invariably on the side of the angels. The strategy relies on the credibility of the brand, and public confidence in the Virgin chairman himself, to "do the right thing." (Incredibly for a businessman, Branson was one of a handful of people chosen in a recent poll of Britain's youth as someone they would trust to "re-write the Ten Commandments.")

"If you go for big, fat, lazy brand leaders, it's often easy to offer better value for money."

In many of the markets Virgin has entered consumers sensed that they were not being treated fairly, but couldn't see any other choice than the big players. They simply accepted that their best interests were not being served. Virgin offers an alternative. As one Virgin executive observes: "If you go for big, fat, lazy brand leaders, it's often easy to offer better value for money."

In addition, it allows you to be on the side of the consumer, who will thank you for it.

Branson's greatest gift as an entrepreneur and a businessman is his preoccupation with the consumers' point of view. When he went into the music business in the 1970s, for example, the long-haired – and later spiky haired – youngsters he was selling to hated the "straight" music establishment, which they believed ripped off fans and artists. They saw Branson as a crusader for their alternative culture.

When he launched Virgin Direct, the financial services company, Branson expressly said that he was going to shake up the market. It was a "dirty business" he said, that needed cleaning up.

> **Branson on financial services:** "The consumer has been taken for a ride for too long by an industry which has been able to hide its charges."

"The Virgin name is trusted, especially by younger people," he said. "The consumer has been taken for a ride for too long by an industry which has been able to hide its charges."[2]

HOIST A PIRATE FLAG

Others see Branson more as a buccaneer than a crusader. The appeal of the swashbuckling Virgin boss, they argue, is his complete lack of respect for figures of authority. This, combined with a gleeful sense of fun, and the pleasure of being an irritant to big business, is what attracts them to his side.

On this reading, he steers a course for the most heavily armed treasure ships, laden with the spoils of excessive market power. Time and time again, he has hoisted the Virgin logo over a new venture like a modern day skull and crossbones, as he and his youthful pirate crew board the market of one multinational or another.

Branson is well aware of this imagery and has used the pirate motif to good effect, to generate publicity and to antagonize the competition, something that he excels at. Shortly after the launch of Virgin Atlantic Airways, for example, Branson issued an invitation to photographers from the British national press to record his swashbuckling antics. The location: Heathrow, London's main airport – where British Airways keeps a full-size model of Concorde decked out in its corporate livery.

At the appointed time, Branson appeared dressed as a buccaneer, complete with eye patch, and lowered the Virgin livery onto Concorde, stealing the UK national carrier's thunder and providing a fantastic photo opportunity. The newspapers the next day carried photographs of Branson and his Virgin pirates boarding the BA flagship. Lord King, BA chairman at the time, was said to be so incensed when he saw the pictures that he almost broke the sound barrier himself.

EVERY UNDERDOG MUST HAVE HIS DAY

Branson is very good at positioning Virgin as the underdog (even though when viewed as a group, Virgin is actually a big company in its own right). It's hard to think badly of a man who picks on companies that are, or at least appear to be, much bigger than his.

Sports fans know that the outsider will often attract the neutral observer to its side. The same seems to work in business. Positioning Virgin as the small guy has important psychological advantages. It plays well with customers, especially those who feel neglected or that they have been taken for a ride in the past. They are likely to be drawn to the plucky, tenacious style of the little guy who is prepared to stand up to the bullies. Faced with the prospect of some cheeky upstart taking on the might of a multinational, neutral onlookers can't help but applaud Virgin's audacity.

It's also good for the motivation of Virgin employees to feel they are taking part in an epic struggle: Virgin's entrepreneurial flair and enthusiasm pitted against lumbering corporate beefcake. As the underdog, they have everything to gain and nothing to lose. At the same time, the arrival of a loud-mouthed "hippy" like Branson on their territory is almost guaranteed to incense the competition – forcing them to make mistakes.

It's clear, too, that there's something in Branson's psyche that responds to the challenge. He delights in having the odds stacked against him, and takes enormous pleasure in doing what the experts say can't be done. Where that challenge involves administering shock treatment to a complacent market leader, it is all the more appealing.

When a Coca-Cola executive boasted that "without our economies of scale and our incredible marketing system, whoever tried to duplicate our product would get nowhere," Branson couldn't wait to have a go.[3]

He also has an instinctive feel for what can be achieved. Of his decision to go into the airline business in 1984, he says: "It was a move which in pure economic terms everybody thought was mad, including my closest friends. But it was something which I felt we could bring something to that others were not bringing."

PICK YOUR BATTLES

The decisions to enter both the airline and cola markets, however, were carefully considered. Although he gives the impression that he likes to climb business mountains simply because "they are there," in almost every case Branson is responding to specific business opportunities that present themselves.

In the case of Virgin Cola, he was approached by a soft drinks company with a high quality cola formula looking for strong brand name; in the case of Virgin Atlantic he was approached by Randolph Fields, a young lawyer who had already done much of the leg work for launching an airline but needed financial backing. Both opportunities were too good to miss.

Sometimes, however, the logic is not clear at first to the so-called experts, a point Branson likes to ram home when he gets the chance. Take the example of Virgin's foray into the UK financial services market.

"We looked long and hard at the marketplace and realized that although there were 600 companies selling PEPs, pensions and the like, they all charged almost identically high prices. There was always an up-front commission (often hidden) a high annual fee and usually a Mr or Mrs Ten Percent sitting in the middle raking off a fat commission. It was like a giant cartel ..."

"The interesting thing here is that when we launched the business, the marketing gurus almost universally cried out the fatal words 'brand stretching', without stopping to think that, in fact, the whole idea was incredibly close to the basic proposition offered by Virgin Atlantic to transatlantic passengers. At its simplest, a quality product with flair at reasonable prices. All they could see was a different product. But the general public, not versed in marketing speak, saw it in much the same way as we did."[4]

But there is another side to picking your battles. If there is one lesson that Richard Branson can teach aspiring entrepreneurs above all others, it is to expect trouble when you go up against big business. There is an old proverb: a gorilla with a gnat on its back has a tendency to try to swat it (all the more so if that gnat is making a lot of noise and has its photograph in the newspapers).

"If you take on established brands, many of whom have near monopolies, you expect everything to be thrown at you to weaken your position. We have had to put up with these sorts of attack for many years. Vast amounts of money are spent spinning stories in an attempt to damage your proposition, or preferably to smother it before it gets established."[5]

Branson on tackling big business:
"If you take on established brands, many of whom have near monopolies, you expect everything to be thrown at you to weaken your position."

Virgin, however, has shown itself to be a robust competitor. There are two factors here. The first is that Branson has never been prepared to let the big guys walk all over him. But second, and just as important, he picks his battles very, very carefully.

Faced with an aggressive competitor, the Branson strategy is simple. Make a lot of noise to irritate him so that he tries to swat you, and then sit back and wait for him to make a mistake. Once he does, hit him hard where it really hurts. This is a technique he has used to good effect on a number of occasions. (It helps to have some excellent lawyers, too.)

HIT 'EM WHERE IT HURTS

In a number of cases, Branson has used guerrilla tactics against a larger rival. When the airline Virgin Atlantic started, promotional activities were targeted to score points off the much larger British Airways. Too small to be a serious competitor at that time, Virgin nevertheless talked a good fight.

The BA management culture at that time can be described as robust if not downright aggressive. At BA's headquarters, Branson was seen as an upstart with rather too much to say for himself. Worse still, he had no experience of running an airline and had identified himself with Freddie Laker, another upstart, whose airline had done much to bring down the prices of transatlantic fares before going bust. A number of cheeky publicity stunts and carefully worded Branson sound bites were bound to get under the skin of the BA management.

What happened next is still unclear. It would appear that a small cadre of managers within BA became incensed by what they regarded as an affront to their company. Apparently, this led to serious errors of judgement, including the use of some sharp competitive practices – or dirty tricks – aimed at undermining Virgin's business. Faced by a serious threat to his airline, and quite possibly the rest of Virgin too, Branson came out fighting.

In the US, he could take advantage of the "excellent anti-trust laws" to pursue BA through the courts. But in Britain he opted to fight on a different battlefield. Knowing full well that the UK competition laws are not as strong, he decided to shame BA publicly.

Branson told the press that BA was waging a dirty tricks campaign against Virgin Atlantic. But the allegations seemed so far-fetched that the British press didn't know quite what to make of them. Finally, however, a documentary maker started to investigate the claims. The resulting programme was called "Violating Virgin," and provided corroborative evidence to back up Branson's claims of a dirty tricks campaign.

When the documentary maker approached BA to comment on his findings, a letter from a BA spokesman claimed: "he had fallen into the trap of being used for Richard Branson's propaganda, which sets out to contrive controversy with British Airways to create publicity for himself and his company and inflict serious damage on the reputation of BA."

In an attempt to reassure its employees, BA then published the letter in its in-house newspaper *BA News*, and the company's media spokesman also drafted a letter for BA's chairman Lord King to send to those who had written to him about the documentary. The letter accused Branson of "continuing to mount a campaign against us through the media" and added "It appears Mr Branson's motivation is to create publicity for himself and his airline."

The competition had just made a mistake, and Richard Branson was about to punish them for it. Citing the letters, Branson issued a writ for libel against BA and its chairman.

In early 1993, British Airways settled the libel action for £610,000 – at the time, the highest sum ever paid in Britain as a libel settlement – plus all legal costs. The final bill was probably over £5 million.

But, as one newspaper noted in 1993: "The Dirty Tricks affair won Branson more than just the £610,000 in damages and public apology from his arch-enemy Lord King. It also boosted his appeal to a public that instinctively backed the small guy over the bullying giant. Now everyone wants a slice of the Branson myth."[6]

More recently, Branson was on the other end of a libel action, but still came out on top. The case was brought against Branson by Guy Snowden, chairman of the American gaming company

GTech, and a member of the board of the UK lottery organizer Camelot. After Branson's own bid to run the UK lottery through a consortium had failed, he alleged that Snowden had tried to bribe him to pull out of the race to run the UK National Lottery. Snowden denied the allegation, and sued Branson for libel.This proved a mistake. One barrister commented that, from the defendant's point of view, Richard Branson is the nightmare plaintiff in a libel case. Of all figures in British public life, he has the purest reputation and is generally well-liked by the public.

With its fondness for heroes and villains, The British press characterized Snowden as a villain; Richard Branson as the people's champion. His high court victory led to Snowden standing down from his post at Camelot. Branson gave the £100,000 damages from the case to charity.

Nicci Gerrard on Branson versus Snowden: "A character from *Chariots of Fire* had defeated a character out of *Goodfellas.*"

One journalist noted at the time that "A character from *Chariots of Fire* had defeated a character out of *Goodfellas.*"[7]

PICK ON SOMEONE BIGGER THAN YOU

Picking on the big guys is almost an article of faith for Virgin, but it also plays an important role in Branson's success. Along with the obvious downsides, attacking dominant market positions has some important upsides. Markets dominated by big players tend to have fat profit margins, with plenty of scope to make money. They also enable Virgin to play the role of the underdog, something that works to its advantage with consumers, employees and the media.

The first lesson of the Branson business strategy is:

◆ Make business a crusade. Branson has a remarkable ability to clothe almost everything he does in a crusading cloak. This lends the Virgin brand moral authority.
◆ Hoist a pirate flag. Others see Branson more as a buccaneer than a crusader. His appeal is seen as a lack of respect for figures of authority, combined with a gleeful sense of fun and the pleasure of being an irritant to big business.
◆ Play the underdog. It's hard to think badly of a man who picks on companies that are, or at least appear to be, bigger than his.
◆ Pick your battles. Although he gives the impression that he likes to climb business mountains simply because "they are there," in almost every case Branson is responding to specific business opportunities that present themselves.
◆ Hit them where it hurts. In a number of cases, Branson has successfully used guerrilla tactics against a larger rival.

NOTES

1   Hoskings, Patrick, writing in the *Independent*.

2   Brown, Mick, *Richard Branson: The Authorized Biography*, 4th edn, Headline, UK, 1998.

3   Mitchell, Alan, *Leadership by Richard Branson*, Amrop International, 1995.

4   Branson, Richard, BBC "Money Programme" lecture, July 1998.

5   Branson, Richard, BBC "Money Programme" lecture, July 1998.

6   Davidson, Andrew, "Virgin's Angel: The rise and rise of Richard Branson," *Sunday Times Magazine*, May 30, 1993.

7   Gerrard, Nicci, "Why do we love Richard Branson," *The Observer*, February 8, 1998.

Two

DO THE HIPPY, HIPPY SHAKE

"When I started, I didn't realize there was a different way to be a businessperson. Now my business is using its credibility and power to make our world a better place to hang out in."
– Ben Cohen, co-founder of Ben & Jerry's Homemade[1]

With his informal style and nonconformist attitude, Richard Branson has been called a "hippy capitalist." A product of the swinging Sixties, his aversion to wearing a suit, in particular, has led to him being linked to other "new age managers" including Anita Roddick of the natural cosmetics company Body Shop and those purveyors of love and ice cream, Ben Cohen and Jerry Greenfield of Ben & Jerry's Homemade.

In the 1960s, Branson marched on the American Embassy in London calling for an end to the Vietnam War – as did many other long-haired young men and women. He also used his magazine *Student* to voice the views of liberal reactionaries such as the actress Vanessa Redgrave. But he was more attracted by the buzz and excitement of London at that time than he ever was to the hippy cause.

In Branson's case the hippy tag is misleading. In reality, his affinity with flower power and the 1960s movement is less a commitment to a hard and fast set of principles or political beliefs, and much more to do with being in tune with the times. This sense of being part of whatever is hip and trendy is one of his greatest business attributes. It has allowed him to project the Virgin brand as a "cool" alternative to whatever the suits are offering.

Branson has always been uncomfortable with the hippy label. More accurately, he is and always has been anti-corporate. He has a healthy disrespect for the hubris and bullshit of big business. In particular he has no time for those who hide behind suits and ties, or for business school graduates who think that managing a business is just about numbers.

Branson on the British business establishment: "Apart from a few exceptions, post-war Britain has bred a domestic commercial culture that is anti-competitive, cartel-based, and patriarchal."

Looking around him at the British business establishment in the 1960s, he didn't much like what he saw. "Apart from a few exceptions, post-war Britain has bred a domestic commercial culture that is anti-competitive, cartel-based, and patriarchal," Branson notes. From the start, he appointed himself as the official debunker of that culture, and has made his fortune by providing an alternative.

Here again, fact and fiction fuse to create an impression of Branson that is teasingly open to interpretation. "A child of the revolutionary 1960s, he's forged a unique synthesis of the youth revolution's values and the needs of a modern business,"[2] says one commentator.

Alternatively, as his biographer Mick Brown observes, he simply "absorbed the idealism of the era and assimilated it into a hazy benevolence, 'to do something for young people' – particularly if that something provided fun, excitement and a challenge for himself."

Branson would have been drawn to whatever was happening at the time. In the 1960s it was inevitable that he would be involved in the hippy scene. His antenna always pick up the latest crackle of energy – and he usually slaps the Virgin brand on the source. In the early 1970s, for example, his record label signed Mike Oldfield and Tangerine Dream. Later, it helped put Punk on the map, signing up the Sex Pistols when the other record labels thought they were too controversial.

As one journalist noted: "it is as if we got it the wrong way round all along. Instead of a hippy entering the world of business; it was a businessman who entered the hippy world (and the Punk world, and then any other gap in the market he happened to see.)"[3]

> "Instead of a hippy entering the world of business; it was a businessman who entered the hippy world (and the Punk world, and then any other gap in the market he happened to see.)"

Branson isn't that interested in politics, although his popularity and influence with younger people mean that politicians beat a path to his door. In the 1980s, he was photographed with Margaret Thatcher. But even though she liked to see him as an exemplar of her policies, the two were never close. More recently, Branson has been linked with Tony Blair's government.

The truth is that he is not particularly interested in ideologies. Pragmatism is the Branson creed, a point reflected in his willingness to work with governments of different shades. At heart, he is left of centre on social issues, but not fanatically so. "I suppose I am left-wing – well only to the extent that I think left-wing views are sane and rational," he told the left-leaning *Guardian* newspaper. "Utopian but almost apolitical" is how one former employee describes him.

DON'T BE A BREAD HEAD

"Money is not his motivation," says a friend who has known Branson for 25 years. "It is not a necessity. He could cope fine without it." And he does, travelling the world without any cash on him. Some see this as the affectation of a millionaire, but others say Branson's only real interest in money is as a way of measuring his achievements. Somehow, too, he's persuaded others that money isn't the most important thing.

Virgin has a long-standing tradition of not overpaying its staff. Many employees have been content to work for less than the going market rate because they enjoy the buzz. (The company also tries to provide a long-term career for those who remain loyal.)

The cousin of one employee who worked on Branson's first commercial venture, for example, recalls his initial impressions of the fledgling entrepreneur. On arriving in Albion Street, where the magazine was based, he was surprised to be greeted by Branson with a kiss. "I thought, Christ, this is odd, but also what an interesting and exciting place to be – because it was a friendly kiss."

It needed to be,[4] because nobody on the magazine's staff was being paid a salary at that time. Many have remarked on Branson's extraordinary knack for getting people to work for little or no financial reward and no other obvious personal advantage. A number put it down to a curiously inspiring sense that it was somehow for the greater good, and in some way furthered the cause of some noble idea. But nobody could ever quite put their finger on what it was. By some ingenious method, Branson convinced these otherwise rational individuals that to forgo financial reward was "fun."

He doesn't like paying big executive salaries either. Even though he has made several of his long-term managers millionaires by giving them a stake in the business, he is canny about using financial carrots, and is astute enough to offer shares in individual businesses worth much less than a stake in the group.

Despite his wealth, Branson's own appetite for material things is surprisingly modest – by billionaire standards, at least. True, he did own a Caribbean Island which is now owned by the Virgin Group, and has several homes around the world, but unlike other very rich men he doesn't flaunt his wealth. He doesn't collect priceless works of art, cars or horses (some rare species of duck at his Oxfordshire home don't really count). He hates shopping for clothes, and is famous for wearing cheap shoes and tasteless jumpers. These days, he prefers to let his wife shop for him.

Sometimes, say those who work with him, he can be arrogant, but he is never flash. He also shows little interest in hanging out with the international jet set – although his interests in the music business mean he bumps into the odd rock star here and there, usually at his own parties. As one Virgin employee observes: "He sees everything as a game. He regards life as a cosmic version of Monopoly."[5]

NO JACKET REQUIRED

Branson's dislike of wearing a suit and tie is legendary and has helped give him and the Virgin brand a distinctive image. These days, the patterned sweaters that are his trademark have been joined by the occasional sports jacket. He even put on a pin-stripe suit and bowler hat to promote Virgin shares when the company was floated, but his idea of power dressing remains resolutely low key.

Here again, though, he is not the hippy people take him for. The young entrepreneur was more nerd than beatnik. "The outsize jumper and untidy haircut, the black, horn-rimmed spectacles, fractured at the bridge and held together with Sellotape, gave him the air of a perpetually genial schoolboy – an air which he has never quite shaken off." Mick Brown, notes in his biography of Branson.[6]

His informal dress sense stands out from the crowd, something that works to his advantage. There is one story that epitomizes his inverse power dressing. In the early days of Virgin, the sight of pony-tailed men and women in jeans and tank tops walking into Coutts, one of the oldest and most conservative British banks, became a regular sight. It was natural therefore that when the company experienced a cash flow crisis that threatened to put it out of business that it should turn to the bank for help.

A meeting was arranged between Branson and the Virgin account manager at Coutts. When the day arrived, the young entrepreneur turned up for work dressed as usual in jeans and T-shirt. "Richard," said one of his colleagues, "don't you think it's time to put a suit on?" The young Branson grinned. "If I suddenly turn up at the bank wearing a suit and tie," he explained, "they will know we're in trouble." In the event, Branson strolled into the meeting in his jeans, and informed his bankers that the business was expanding so quickly that he needed a bigger overdraft to keep up with orders. The bank took one look at the scruffy, self-assured youth and agreed.

Andrew Davidson, a journalist who interviewed Branson, tells another story that sums up the Virgin chairman's attitude to the stuffy British business establishment.[7] Due to give a speech at the Institute of Directors' annual conference at the Royal Albert Hall, Branson was answering questions in a makeshift office in his Holland Park home, wearing grey slacks, cheap black shoes and a hand-knitted sweater. Then from the room next door, his assistant enquires about the whereabouts of his suit. He groans. "Do I have to wear a suit?"

"Without thinking," Davidson says, "I tell him how years ago, I was once thrown out of the Institute of Directors for forgetting to wear a tie. It's like a red rag to a bull. 'Right, that's settled,' Branson shouts through to his assistant in the next room. 'No suit, Penni. I'm going as I am.' He knows that, as he is giving one of the keynote speeches, he is hardly likely to be turned away."

POWER TO THE PEOPLE

One area where Branson's sixties credentials are genuine is in his treatment of the people who work for him. Branson is a great believer in people power. He has built the Virgin brand on the premise that people – customers and employees – come first. He is a product of the democratizing ideals of the Sixties and has an instinctive sense that all people should be treated

with respect. Today, companies everywhere are busy disman-
tling their hierarchies and eliminating the outward signs of
executive privilege. In eschewing the trappings of status and
power from the start, Branson was way ahead of the game.

Branson likes to refer to Virgin employees as belonging to a
large extended family. In the early years of Virgin, every new
employee was given Branson's home telephone number, and
encouraged to call if they had any bright ideas – or complaints.
To this day, everyone in the company calls him by his first name.

It is typical of Branson, too, that when his Virgin Megastore
opened in New York, the invitation list included the crews of all
Virgin Atlantic aircraft that happened to be in town that night.
Another classic Branson touch was to share out the £610,000
settlement from British Airways from the dirty tricks libel case.
The money was divided equally between all Virgin staff. Each
employee received £166 – known as the "BA Bonus." It sent a
message that together they had all won a great victory.

Branson believes in keeping faith with his staff in good times
and in bad. Employees who lose their jobs can appeal directly
to the chairman, who has been known to intervene personally
if he thinks the appeal is justified. Even when the airline business was depressed by the Gulf War and the recession of the
early 1990s, Virgin Atlantic was anxious to avoid redundan-
cies, and managed to avoid laying off any staff between 1991
and 1993.

"We tried to look for every way round that," says Branson.
"Some went off on half-paid leave with the understanding that
if they wanted their jobs back when business picked up they
could have them."

Interestingly, he has made a virtue of the fact that he retains ownership of the majority share of the Virgin empire to protect employees. His decision to take the company back into private ownership after it was floated on the London Stock market, he claims, gives him more freedom to be a caring boss.

"The point is that as a private company, you can make decisions which a public company finds more difficult. Staff should come first; if it means making £5 million less, then that is the right decision to make. It's like a family. When people use the word family with regard to companies it is often extremely misused. But if the going was tough, I would never throw my children out. Everyone just shares a bit less. It should be exactly the same with a company."[8]

Branson on the interests of employees: "Staff should come first; if it means making £5 million less, then that is the right decision to make."

SEX AND DRUGS AND ROCK 'N' ROLL

From the start, the Virgin business was run on a deliberate policy of mixing business with pleasure. From its earliest days, the Virgin philosophy has been work hard, play hard. For years, the entire staff of the record company, publishing company, and studio management team would spend weekends away together at the company's expense. Starting on a Friday and ending on a Sunday night, they would decamp to a country hotel.

As Tim Jackson notes in his book *Virgin King*: "Attendance was in theory optional, but those who did not come were told jokingly that they were expected to spend the weekend working in the office."

"At the hotel, other record companies might fill the days with talk of sales targets or new products. At Virgin, business was banned. Instead, the guests would spend the weekend playing tennis or golf, swimming and sunning themselves, eating and drinking with great gusto, and taking a few drugs and sleeping with each other in the evenings."[9]

It was typical of Branson, too, that when *Mayfair* magazine unearthed some nude pictures of his wife Joan taken a decade or so earlier, he took it in his stride. Where other millionaire tycoons might have tried to prevent the magazine publishing the pictures, Branson was delighted that the world should know how beautiful the mother of his children was.[10] When a Virgin employee later teased him about the pictures, Branson retorted that he had asked the magazine for full-color enlargements and planned to put them on the wall over his bed.

The offices of *Student*, Branson's first business venture after leaving school, are said to have resembled a hippy commune more than a magazine office. Deadlines slipped, the publication lost money and eventually failed, but the people working on the publication had a good time. Where other companies might hold "brain storming sessions," staff at the magazine were more likely to sit around and get stoned.

Branson's next project was more successful, but the attitude was the same. According to one source: "The new enterprise –

a mail order record company – was conducted in an atmosphere filled with marijuana smoke.[11] The first order of the day was to roll joints. The company's inspired name was conceived during one such session."

(Whether Branson himself actually inhaled is difficult to say. But on a recent BBC television programme,[12] he was asked whether there was any product that the Virgin name would never be used to brand. He sensibly ducked the question, but offered the thought that if legalized Virgin would be more likely to put its logo on cannabis cigarettes than it would on tobacco.)

Rock 'n' roll, meanwhile, was paying the bills. Not only did the company go on to open a number of record stores, by the 1970s the Virgin record label was making a serious contribution at source – discovering the likes of Mike Oldfield, Tangerine Dream, and Boy George, and signing the Sex Pistols. It even attempted to sign those masters of the rock 'n' roll lifestyle, the Rolling Stones. (The profits from Mike Oldfield's *Tubular Bells* and to a lesser extent Tangerine Dream's album *Phaedra* bankrolled the entire Virgin enterprise and expansion for three years after their release. Later, the revenue from sales of Culture Club's records made a major contribution to the Virgin coffers – releasing vast reservoirs of cash into the struggling Virgin empire.)

Despite its size, the social aspect of the business remains important to this day. Each year, Branson hosts a series of parties at his home for all the Virgin employees – everyone from senior managers to airline crew, shop assistants to aero-engineers, and soft drinks experts to secretaries. There they are lavishly entertained with a fun-fair, barbecues, bouncy castles, punting on the nearby river and other activities. It is a Virgin tradition, too, that Branson himself ends up in the water at least a couple of times in the course of the weekend.

As Mick Brown says in his biography of Branson: "One is hard put to think of any other business man or captain of industry in any field – Lord Hanson or Donald Trump, Alan Sugar or Bill Gates – who would entertain his staff like this. Equally it is hard to think of another chairman of an airline who would greet his passengers at the door of the aircraft, or dress up in full drag as a stewardess to serve them in-flight drinks."

(Actually, on the second count, Herb Kelleher of Southwest Airlines springs to mind. Branson would approve; he is a Herb fan.)

SHAKE IT UP BABY

Another common denominator of business Branson-style is the desire to shake up the markets he enters – and the establishment in general. The sectors where Virgin has set up its stall are rarely ever the same again. It is intrinsic to the rebellious Branson approach to pick sectors that are crying out for innovation. Often, they are characterized by a lack of imagination and a lack of responsiveness to the real needs of customers. In some cases, the sad state of affairs is almost accepted by consumers as simply "the way it is." Then along comes Branson and says, "it doesn't have to be this way."

A classic example was Virgin's entry into the UK financial services markct. It was hard to imagine anything more incongruous

than the pirates of Virgin talking about pensions and investment plans. Yet, once it became clear they were serious, nothing
seemed more natural: Virgin, the company with serious street
cred, offering young people an alternative to the stuffy bankers and insurance companies by providing a no nonsense, no
bullshit approach to financial services.

To identify the opportunity, however, it took someone who knew
how the financial community worked but wasn't part of it. Rowan
Gormley had joined Virgin from a venture capital company in
1991. For several years he had worked with Branson sifting
through the hundreds of business proposals the company receives. He knew the Virgin formula. It was Gormley who
approached his boss with the idea that Virgin should get involved in pensions and life insurance.

Initially, though, even Branson thought this was going too far.
At the age of 46, he had never had a pension in his life – and
with his millions was unlikely ever to need one. His fortune,
after all, was built on risk-taking. Besides, there was nothing
sexy or fun about pensions.

But Gormley argued his case from another stand point. A huge
amount of the payments people made for pensions and life
insurance went on administrative charges and overheads, he
pointed out. Fund management and investment companies also
charged huge commissions for handling customers' money. But
a number of new ventures including Direct Line and First Direct had shown that direct banking and insurance via the
telephone rather than high street branches was a viable model
in the UK.

There was an added appeal, too. Branson's brush with the stock market when Virgin was listed had reinforced a suspicion of the investment community. Fund managers who decided which shares to buy and sell were arrogant and often ill-informed about the real value and priorities of the companies they traded in. Gormley confirmed the point, explaining that simply tracking the FTSE index was likely to be more financially rewarding than investing in a managed fund. Virgin, then, should launch an index tracking PEP (Personal Equity Plan).

Within the investment community, index linked funds, he told Branson, had been a well-kept secret for years, partly because they had been shown regularly to outperform investment fund managers. With an index tracking PEP, linked to the performance of the best companies on the stock exchange, investors could play the stock market without the hassle and high commissions of brokers or fund managers. It would shake up the industry. This appealed to Branson.

What at first sight had seemed an unlikely venture was in fact a gaping hole in the market. It simply took the Virgin angle on things to see it for what it was. (Recent reports that the senior management at Virgin Direct is concerned that Branson may not be the right person to promote financial products and should be distanced from the company suggest that perhaps they "don't get it" after all. The whole point is that Richard Branson is not a banker or an accountant – or even a "grown up" in the conventional sense of the term – and nor are most of Virgin Direct's customers. It is because they like to think that they have something in common with the Virgin chairman that the Virgin name appeals, and also because they trust him personally.)

"I can't walk past a fat and complacent business sector without wanting to shake it up a bit," Branson said, on the launch of Virgin Direct. He was banking on the Virgin name, he said, to allay the distrust that ordinary people have traditionally felt for City and Wall Street types.

Branson on the launch of Virgin Direct: "I can't walk past a fat and complacent business sector without wanting to shake it up a bit."

The Virgin PEP quickly became the fastest-selling product in the financial market. In its first year, Virgin Direct had sold £400 million of PEPs to 75,000 investors. By the end of 1997, 200,000 people had invested in the scheme and more than £1 billion was under Virgin Direct management. Branson's next target would be personal banking. The financial services market would never be quite the same again.

DO THE HIPPY, HIPPY SHAKE

With his informal style and nonconformist attitude, Richard Branson has been called a "hippy capitalist." A hippy he's not, but Branson's alternative management style offers the following lessons to those who aspire to make money not war:

◆ Don't be a bread head – there's more to business than just money. Despite his wealth, Branson's own appetite for material things is surprisingly modest. Somehow, too, he persuades others that money isn't the most important thing.

◆ Dress down every day (not just Fridays). Branson's dislike of wearing a suit and tie is legendary. His informal dress sense stands out from the crowd, something that works to his advantage.

◆ Put people first. Branson is a great believer in people power. He has built the Virgin brand on the premise that people – customers and employees – come first.

◆ Everybody must get stoned. From the start, the Virgin business was run on a deliberate policy of mixing business with pleasure. From its earliest days, the Virgin philosophy has been work hard, play hard.

◆ Don't imitate, innovate. Another common denominator of business Branson-style is the desire to shake up the markets he enters – and the establishment in general. The sectors where Virgin has set up its stall are rarely ever the same again.

NOTES

1   Ben Cohen, *The Globe and Mail*, May 1988.
2   Mitchell, Alan, *Leadership by Richard Branson*, Amrop International, 1995.
3   Gerrard, Nicci, "Why do we love Richard Branson?" *The Observer*, February 8, 1998.
4   Brown, Mick, *Richard Branson: The Authorized Biography*, 4th edn, Headline, 1998.
5   Mitchell, Alan, *Leadership by Richard Branson*, Amrop International, 1995.
6   Brown, Mick, *Richard Branson: The Authorized Biography*, 4th edn, Headline, 1998.
7   Davidson, Andrew, "Virgin angel: the rise and rise of Richard Branson," *Sunday Times Magazine*, May 30, 1993.
8   Davidson, Andrew, "Virgin angel: the rise and rise of Richard Branson," *Sunday Times Magazine*, May 30, 1993.
9   Jackson, Tim, *Virgin King*, HarperCollins, London, 1994, p. 51.
10 Jackson, Tim, *Virgin King*, HarperCollins, London, 1994, p. 173.
11 Rodgers, Paul, 'The Branson Phenomenon', *Enterprise* magazine, March/April 1997.
12 "The Money Programme," BBC, July 1998.

Three

HAGGLE: EVERYTHING'S NEGOTIABLE

"… He had a street trader's aptitude for negotiation, knowing exactly when to talk and when to stay silent, when to press his counterpart on a point and when simply to walk away."
–Tim Jackson, author of *Virgin King*

One of Richard Branson's less well known talents is a razor-sharp negotiating technique. Nice guys, so the saying goes, finish last but not Branson. Despite – or perhaps because of – his Mr Nice Guy image, Branson rarely comes out second best in any of the deals he makes. Charisma and an affable charm belie a calculating business brain.

It is no coincidence that of the business partners who have negotiated favorable terms with Branson, a number preferred to conduct negotiations through their lawyers rather than strike a deal with him face-to-face. These include Branson's own cousin Simon Draper who was responsible for signing many of Virgin's musical discoveries including Culture Club.

It is not that Branson is intimidating – quite the opposite; in fact, he is a model of affability. But what those who know him recognize is that his easygoing style hides a shrewd business mind and a fiercely competitive nature. These attributes are complemented by an appetite for haggling that would put a Turkish carpet salesman to shame.

This is combined with surprising patience in one normally so impulsive, and the ability to persuade others that what they are being offered isn't just very reasonable but is actually the better side of the bargain. Often, too, there is a strong element of cheek involved; Branson has no embarrassment in asking for far more than anyone else would dare.

NICE GUYS FINISH FIRST

Ask yourself this: when most entrepreneurs end up giving away larger and larger shares in their businesses in order to secure additional investment to grow, how did Branson grow his empire and end up with a larger share of the group? In 1973, Branson owned 60 percent of the main Virgin holding company; by 1995, he and his family owned 60 percent of a much expanded Virgin empire worth in excess of £1 billion.

That he has achieved this remarkable feat is a testament to his shrewd negotiating skills and persuasive tongue. What Branson is very good at is realizing where the value of a deal really lies and using other elements as bargaining chips. The fact that Virgin is a web of mainly small with a few not-so-small businesses is a great advantage here. He realized long ago that offering a large percentage of a small business is infinitely preferable to giving away shares in the group as a whole.

But the "atomized empire" is just one factor. Tim Jackson, author of the unofficial biography of Branson *Virgin King*, notes a contrast between Branson's private style and his expansive public persona. He observes: "When there was business to be done, Branson loved to haggle; he had a street trader's aptitude for negotiation, knowing exactly when to talk and when to stay silent, when to press his counterpart on a point and when simply to walk away."

> **"When there was business to be done, Branson loved to haggle; he had a street trader's aptitude for negotiation."**

There is to Branson, too, a highly competitive streak, which is always looking to gain the advantage. This is vital for any entrepreneur of serious ambitions and should be cultivated by the up-and-coming tycoon. In Branson's case, it is accentuated by a number of other characteristics. Most important of these is an easy charm that lulls all but the most hardened of negotiators into dropping their guard.

Branson's great skill as a negotiator is one of those happy (for him) accidents of birth. Nature in all its wisdom saw fit to bestow a market trader's mind on a middle-class and seemingly easygoing son of a barrister. Not only does Branson possess the wherewithal to strike a mean deal, it is part of his psyche. Were English public schools less interested in competing at cricket and rugby and rather more in instilling commercial *nous* in their pupils, they might consider inter-school negotiating matches. In that unlikely event, Richard Branson might have captained his school.

One story illustrates Branson's mischievous delight in negotiating. In the early days of the mail order record business, a man telephoned to offer the company some bootlegged Jimi Hendrix records. The caller was told to drop by at the company's offices the next day to discuss the deal with a Mr Zimmerman. When the man turned up at 10 a.m. it was to be told by an earnest Richard Branson that Mr Zimmerman was at a café just around the corner.

When the man returned some time later to report that Mr Zimmerman had not turned up, Branson expressed surprise and innocently asked what it was he wanted to see him about. The man explained that he was going to sell him some records for £1 apiece. "I'll give you 50p each," the artful Branson said, and a deal was struck. Within days, they were sold to devoted Jimi Hendrix fans by mail order at £3 each.

CHEEK OF THE DEVIL

Whenever he is negotiating Branson expects to haggle, always putting in a lower – and sometimes significantly lower – offer. On large purchases – country mansions, aircraft, a Caribbean island – that can make a very big difference. Funnily enough, many business people, especially those who have spent their working lives within large corporations, don't expect to come up against a market trader mentality, a man who will haggle for the sheer pleasure of it.

Branson's brilliant negotiating skills also partly explain why Virgin has done so well from joint ventures and other partnership arrangements. His cheek of the devil negotiating skill has become a hallmark of the company. "No," "never," and "impossible" are not words in the Branson business dictionary.

"When the company was small and he was striking agreements on his own, Branson had enough cheek to demand far more than he ever hoped to win – but also enough patience to argue a deal point by tiny point if the adversary so demanded," notes Tim Jackson. "He was highly skilful at hiding behind others, telling those he was negotiating with that it was the objections of his lawyers or his colleagues, rather than his own misgivings, that made him unable to agree to a proposal."

On many occasions, too, Branson's ability to cajole others into doing what he wants has enabled him to make things happen that might otherwise have been impossible. Branson is especially good at cutting through red tape. During the preparations for one of his hot air balloon record attempts, for example, Branson was informed that a vital test on the prototype balloon could not be carried out because the aerospace company that owned the test chamber had booked it out to other customers every day for the next two years. Branson demanded the name and telephone number of the chairman of the company. Two hours later he called back to say that not only was the chamber now immediately available, but that as a goodwill gesture, the normal charge of £25,000 would be waived.

TALK SOFTLY AND CARRY A BIG STICK

For all his bonhomie, there are those who say that Richard Branson isn't nearly so nice to do business with as you might think. This is a curious view of one of the most successful businessmen this century. It would be naïve to think otherwise. Anyone considering going into business with Virgin should ask themselves a few simple – and rather obvious – questions.

For example: is this the same Richard Branson who after three decades remains the unchallenged leader of one of the best known companies in the world – and still owns about 60 percent of the equity? Is this the same Richard Branson who has taken market share from some of the most aggressive companies in the world?

The point to understand here is that this is no pussycat we're talking about. It would be foolish to think otherwise. You don't get to be where Branson is without a hard edge to your deal making. When Randolph Fields, a young lawyer, brought Branson the idea for Virgin Atlantic Airways, the original agreement was that both men would own half the airline. During the negotiations before the airline's launch, however, Branson forced Fields to accept a 25 percent share; later the same year, Fields was forced to step down as chairman of Virgin Atlantic. A year later Branson bought out Field's stake for £1 million.[1]

Branson has a well-developed sense of where the power lies in a bargaining situation. On occasion, he has been known to press home the advantage when he knows he holds the better hand. That, as they say, is business. Anyone who thinks Virgin is a charity should think again.

> Anyone who thinks Virgin is a charity should think again.

ACTING ON GOOD ADVICE

While Branson himself seems to float from one business adventure to another, he relies on the advice of others with their feet firmly on the ground. Behind Branson's happy-go-lucky public image lurks not just a calculating businessman, but one who knows very well the value of good professional advisers.

> Branson may not be an accountant, but he has always surrounded himself with people who can do the sums.

"I'm not good with figures," he says. "I failed my elementary maths exam."[2]

He may not be an accountant, but he has always surrounded himself with people who can do the sums. Ever since his scrape with the British tax authorities in the early 1970s, which nearly landed him in jail, he has relied on having top-notch accountants, lawyers and merchant bankers helping him dot the "i"s and cross the "t"s of his deals.

Within the Virgin Group, he has also always made sure that there was a team of hard-nosed executives to follow through and tie up any loose ends. Among them are Virgin Group's CEO David Abbott, an accountant by training and long-term Branson aid, and Don Cruikshank, the former McKinsey & Co. consultant who came in to get Virgin ready for privatization and went on to head up Oftel, the UK telecommunications regulatory body.

Some people have even gone so far as to suggest that Branson is more in thrall to his advisers than even Virgin insiders realize. A number of business partners have been irritated by Branson's refusal to be tied down in a contract, and his infuriating habit of renegotiating terms.

One disgruntled businessman went so far as to claim that much of the Virgin phenomenon is the product of a "magnificent manipulation" by "an impenetrable inner sanctum at the centre of the Virgin empire."

If so, it would have to be a remarkable one that could pull the strings of someone as wilful as Richard Branson.

SILVER LININGS

But there is another aspect to Branson the deal maker. When it comes to setup costs, most canny entrepreneurs seek to cover the downside risk. Branson, on the other hand, wants to cover the upside, too. In his mind, every cloud could have a silver-plated lining.

In 1984, for example, Virgin was in the throes of setting up Virgin Atlantic. The first task was to acquire an aircraft. Boeing had a slightly used 747 standing idle in the Arizona desert. Branson was quite sure that he didn't want to own the aircraft outright (he'd seen what happened to Freddie Laker when he tried to buy aircraft) but nor did he want to incur heavy penalties if the airline didn't get off the ground. The deal that was put together by Virgin's lawyers was not a straightforward one.[3]

The jumbo would be bought from Boeing by Barclays Bank, which would then be able to claim the tax allowances for the aircraft's depreciation. Barclays would then lease it to a subsidiary of the Chemical bank of New York, which in turn would lease it to Virgin Atlantic.

New, the aircraft would have cost around $100 million, but the price negotiated by Branson's partner Randolph Fields was $27.8 million. By all accounts it was a good deal, especially since Boeing promised to buy it back for $25 million after a year or two if Virgin wanted. But not good enough for the Virgin chairman. Branson was adamant that Virgin should be able to benefit from the upside if aircraft prices should rise. At his insistence, it was agreed that Boeing would have to pay the market price for it if Virgin decided to sell.

HAGGLE: EVERYTHING'S NEGOTIABLE

One of Richard Branson's less well known talents is a razor-sharp negotiating technique. Despite – or perhaps because of – his Mr Nice Guy image, Branson rarely comes out second best in any of the deals he makes. Charisma and an affable charm belie a calculating business brain. The lessons from the Branson school of negotiating are:

◆ Nice guys finish first. Branson's shrewd negotiating skills and persuasive tongue are accentuated by an easy charm that lulls all but the most hardened of negotiators into dropping their guard.

◆ Never take no for an answer. Branson's cheek of the devil negotiating skill has become a hallmark of the company. "No," "never," and "impossible" are not words in the Branson business dictionary.

◆ Talk softly and carry a big stick. For all his bonhomie, there are those who say that Richard Branson isn't nearly so nice to do business with as you might think. This is a curious view of one of the most successful businessmen this century. It would be naïve to think otherwise.

◆ Get good professional advice. Behind Branson's happy-go-lucky public image lurks not just a calculating businessman, but one who knows very well the value of good professional advisers.

◆ Always cover the upside. When it comes to setup costs, most canny entrepreneurs seek to cover the downside risk. Branson, on the other hand, wants to cover the upside, too. In his mind, every cloud could have a silver-plated lining.

NOTES

1   Jackson, Tim, *Virgin King*, HarperCollins, London, 1994, p. 16.

2   Branson, Richard, "Money Programme," BBC, July 1998.

3   Jackson, Tim, *Virgin King*, HarperCollins, London, 1994.

Four

MAKE WORK FUN

"He captivates the public and employees by the unexpected prospect of making the grey world of work sparkle with fun and excitement."
– Alan Mitchell, from *Leadership by Richard Branson*

Business, in Richard Branson's view, should be fun. This is an important factor both in Branson's own appetite for work and the success of his ventures. Creating an exciting work culture is the best way to motivate and retain good people; it also means you don't have to pay them as much. This is a useful asset, especially if you don't have a reputation as a brilliant inventor, or management visionary, to fall back on. It's all very well being clever, but all work and no play makes Jack a dull boy. Not Richard.

Unlike the computer whiz-kids Bill Gates and Steve Jobs, Branson has never invented any product of a revolutionary nature. Nor does he have the corporate kudos of a Jack Welch, CEO of GE, credited with turning the company around. Branson's achievement is actually more difficult to explain. All the industries he has succeeded in are conventional ones with little in common except that they are mature and dominated by large players. So what is it that Richard Branson knows about business that other people who have been in these conventional industries for years have failed to grasp? More to the point, what does Branson do that they do not?

The answer is Branson inspires people. Because he inspires them, he has the ability to motivate those who work with him and push them to the limit. He possesses a remarkable ability to enable others to achieve what they didn't know they were capable of. What Branson is really good at is creating energy around a goal – be it a business venture or a world record attempt. He exudes confidence and a belief that no mountain is too high to climb. Curiously enough, people seem to like that even more than money (for a while anyway).

ARE WE HAVING FUN YET?

Throughout his business life Branson has managed to portray work as a social activity. Going to the office at Virgin isn't the drudgery that it can be at other companies, or at least, that's what Branson wants his people to believe and clearly believes himself. "I get the best people, I ask questions, and then I say: 'let's have some fun'," he explains.[1]

Branson on the office environment: "I get the best people, I ask questions, and then I say:'let's have some fun'."

In the early days, low wages and run-down work environments were compensated for by regular wild parties and a carnival atmosphere. Even today, the line between working life and social life is hard to draw at the company. Virgin staff work hard and play hard.

There is method in the madness. When you blur the divide between work and play as Branson does, you begin to break down the divide between what matters to people in their private lives and what happens at work. People don't resent working long hours if they believe that they are achieving something for themselves and the people they care about.

Another important aspect of the Virgin culture is its cheeky sense of humor – something that extends to its brand values. Branson himself has a reputation for playing schoolboy pranks of the not-so-subtle kind. Stories of his antics are legion.

On one occasion, so the story goes, he thought it would be entertaining to play a trick on one of his senior managers and closest advisers who was away for a few days. The plan was to sneak into the manager's home at night and remove all his furniture and personal belongings so that when he arrived home he would think he'd been burgled.

What Branson didn't know, however, was that his plan had been tumbled, and arrangements made to turn the joke on him. On his arrival at the address, he was met by the police, who arrested the protesting Virgin boss and locked him up for the night. In the morning, the entire Virgin staff went down to the police station to bail him out. His release was greeted with loud applause.

Branson's sense of humor has landed him in trouble on other occasions, too. One of his trademark party tricks is to seize hold of glamorous guests and turn them upside down. Ivana Trump, former wife of the American billionaire businessman Donald Trump, still hasn't forgiven Branson for hanging her upside down over a swimming pool in front of hundreds of guests at a black-tie party.

The story of his 1992 meeting with the late Sir James Goldsmith shows that he just can't help himself sometimes. Two more different tycoons than Branson and Goldsmith would be hard to imagine. Branson the hippy, who built his empire by growing his own businesses, meets Goldsmith, the corporate raider and takeover baron. Invited to Goldsmith's retreat in Mexico, Branson pushed the billionaire into the swimming pool on the first morning – after promising not to – and was promptly asked to leave. Joan Branson's only comment was "Thank God."[2]

The story shows Branson's reckless disregard for the business establishment. (Others have observed that it was an outstanding example of man management.)

LET 'EM LOOSE

He has always been prepared to hire bright young people with no proven track record, and let them loose on projects. In the early days of Virgin Music, the record label, for example, Branson was happy to take people who had little formal experience of the industry but had a real love of music and passion for making records. Unsupervised, they would put huge effort and energy into their work – to justify the company's belief in them. It was common in those days for staff at the company to turn down job offers from other companies that would have doubled their salaries. The reason? They enjoyed working at Virgin so much.

Empowerment – delegating decision-making authority to staff lower down the organization – became fashionable with management gurus in the 1980s; it has always been in vogue at Virgin. From the very beginning, Branson has surrounded himself with talented people and given them the freedom to be creative. Time and time again, they have rewarded his confidence with dazzling results.

Take the example of Simon Draper, Branson's South African cousin and long-time head of the Virgin record label. Draper it was who spotted many of Virgin's greatest musical discoveries, including Mike Oldfield, Tangerine Dream and Culture Club. Yet when he joined the company he had no formal training or experience, just his enthusiasm for music to guide him. On occasions, too, Draper had to tell Branson why a certain artist would not fit with the label's *avante garde* image. For many years, Virgin Music, due largely to Draper's freedom to sign the artists he wanted, bankrolled the entire Virgin empire.

A similar approach cascades down the organization, with Virgin employees typically having far more discretionary power than staff in other companies at the same level. Virgin Atlantic cabin crew are much more likely to use their initiative than those from certain other airlines who have to follow company dictat to the letter.

Branson uses the physical environment at work to reinforce the Virgin culture. The companies that make up the group are located in buildings – big houses rather than office blocks – that resonate with informality. They have been likened to "hippy hideouts."[3]

Branson also uses an unorthodox "loose" organizational structure to give employees free rein. Virgin is made up of a cluster of small companies that operate independently of each other. This creates more freedom for maneuver. Employees often work harder in small entrepreneurial groups where the wholehearted contribution of everyone is vital to the success of all. There is no room for coasting or passengers at Virgin.

Because they are in friendly competition with other parts of the group too, the different Virgin businesses are encouraged to behave in a more entrepreneurial manner. This also restricts interference from the centre, making it more difficult for senior Virgin executives (apart from Branson) to meddle. In this way he has created the classic "divide and rule" model, which allows him to give his people their heads but maintain absolute control whilst also preserving his cult-like status.

CALL ME RICHARD

To the average Virgin employee, Branson, the company's chairman and major shareholder, is simply Richard. The secret with people, he says, is to praise rather than criticize (something he says applies to bringing up children, too: "Children and companies flourish under praise"[4]).

Branson on people management: "Children and companies flourish under praise."

In the early days of Virgin, when employees wanted to form a trades union, Branson is said to have been truly hurt. He wanted all his employees to be able to discuss problems with him personally. Above all, he wants people to trust him.

Visitors to his office in Holland Park have remarked that he is uncommonly courteous to the people who work with him. He works his staff hard, but unlike many other company chairmen he has resisted the temptation to order his secretaries and assistants around as if they were servants. He is famously approachable, and people calling his office are as likely to find themselves talking directly to Branson as they are to a secretary or assistant.

As Simon Lester, managing director of Cott Europe, the company that provided the original formula and expertise for Virgin Cola, explains: "He is really quite an extraordinary fellow. He continually surprises you with his behavior. When he first called,

he telephoned through directly: no secretary; no normal corporate blockages, which immediately knocks you off your stride
and makes you think, how unusual, how different.

"And when you meet him, you expect to meet this unbeliev-
able, powerful modern day icon, and he's just the most
charming individual in a very ordinary way. He stutters a fair
amount. He is not a power monger. He is just a really nice guy.
And underneath you know he is one of the most determined
and energetic people that you could possibly wish to meet."

It is his lack of front that has enabled Branson, the public schoolboy of privileged upbringing, to court the adoration of his staff
as well as the general public. His popularity crosses class barriers. But it goes deeper than that. People see in Branson a
business leader who is motivated by a higher purpose; someone who embodies a set of values and is prepared to stand up
and be counted. This is an image Branson cultivates as it provides the ideal counterbalance to the frivolous fun and games.

NO PAIN, NO GAIN

Parties and pranks are no substitute for hard work, of course.
What they do achieve is to set the mood and culture of Virgin.
The other side of the equation is creating a sense of challenge.
By inspiring his staff, Branson gets exceptional performance
from them, with sales and profit levels far above industry standards. Here, the way the Virgin empire is structured is
important.

Branson explains: "When a company gets to a certain size, instead of letting it grow bigger and bigger and putting it into

bigger and bigger offices, I will take, say, the assistant market-ing manager, the assistant managing director, the assistant sales manager, and I'll say: you're now the manager of a new com-pany. This was the case with Virgin records which was eventually divided into five companies."[5]

This policy of promoting talented people from within encour-ages Virgin staff to give their all in the hope that they will be noticed by the company's chairman and given an opportunity really to shine. But another anecdote shows another side to Branson: the master motivator, pushing his employees to their limits.

Branson likes to attempt the impossible. On one occasion he telephoned the marketing director of Virgin Atlantic and asked him to place an ad in the London *Evening Standard*, only to be told that it was too late, and that they had missed the newspaper's copy deadlines. Branson insisted that his market-ing manager do his best all the same. The skeptical employee spent the entire morning on the telephone. Through a super-human effort on all sides, an ad did just make the last edition of the *Standard*. On hearing this, Branson thanked his market-ing manager for his efforts; but there was an unmistakable note of triumph in his voice as he did so.[6]

The message is clear. Branson wants and expects the people around him to do their best to achieve whatever goals he sets, rather than argue over whether something can or cannot be done. But then, doing the impossible is part of the Virgin cul-ture, something that is reinforced by Branson's own record-breaking feats and derring-do in speed boats and hot air balloons.

THE MAGICAL MYSTERY TOUR

Part of the appeal of Virgin as an employer and as a consumer brand is the promise of an adventure to be had. Everything about its larger-than-life founder resonates with the "Boy's Own" heroes from children's stories. Part Biggles and part pirate, Branson bristles with fun and adventure – something he has brought to every industry Virgin has entered.

There is, too, an aura of excitement about doing something new. "What I like most of all is to learn," Branson says. "When I feel that I've learnt what there is to know about telecommunications, or airlines, or cosmetics – well you name it – then I move on to something else. It's like being at university, which I never went to, and taking crash courses."[7]

The whole Virgin phenomenon, for him, is a magical mystery tour. It's a journey that has already lasted 30 years. If Virgin went bankrupt – "and it did nearly go bankrupt during the dirty tricks time, and that's why I had to sell the record company" he says – he wouldn't mind so much. "I would pack up my bag and take the family on an adventure. South America. I've never been to South America. It would be fun."

But as more and more people get on the bus, the pressure on the driver to take them somewhere different – somewhere fun, but also somewhere uplifting and unspoiled by the excesses of capitalism – increases.

To date, Branson has persuaded customers and employees to board the Virgin tour bus simply because it offered an adventure that was something different to what the suits were offering.

In the future he may find that passengers expect him to have a destination in mind – a kinder, more caring version of what business is for, perhaps. This legacy seems to occupy him more than it used to.

Increasingly, he seems to sense that some sort of explanation of where the adventure might lead is expected of him. This is starting to show in his rhetoric. The great question for Branson is where now for his vision of business? Will Virgin simply crumble to dust when he vacates the premises, or has he built a lasting monument to a new form of capitalism?

The brash adventurer is being asked to put his telescope to his good eye and tell the world what he sees just over the horizon. Branson is starting to think about what it all means, and his place in history.

He is an admirer of what he regards as other like-minded businesses. He detects a kindred spirit at the famously eccentric Southwest Airlines. As he recently explained: "Southwest employees have bought into the company for the principles for which the airline stands. A piece of legislation that advocates higher landing fees, for example, isn't seen just as an affront to their profitability; it's also an affront to their idealism. They are firmly entrenched in the idea that profitability is the precursor to job security, shareholder return, and investment in the community. They are in the business to make a difference. This is what a brand should stand for."[8]

MAKE WORK FUN

Business, in Richard Branson's view, should be fun. Creating an exciting work culture is the best way to motivate and retain good people; it also means you don't have to pay them as much. The Branson technique for managing people provides the following lessons:

◆ It pays to play. Going to the office at Virgin isn't the drudgery that it can be at other companies, or at least that's what Branson wants his people to believe and clearly believes himself.

◆ Let employees loose. Branson has always surrounded himself with talented people and given them the freedom to be creative. Time and time again, they have rewarded his confidence with dazzling results.

◆ Encourage informality – stay on first name terms. To the average Virgin employee, Branson, the company's chairman and major shareholder, is simply "Richard."

◆ Enthusiasm is infectious. By inspiring his staff, Branson gets exceptional performance from them, with sales and profit levels far above industry standards.

◆ Make business an adventure. Part of the appeal of Virgin as an employer and as a consumer brand is the promise of an adventure to be had.

NOTES

1   Gerrard, Nicci, "Why do we love Richard Branson?" *The Observer*, February 8, 1998.
2   Davidson, Andrew, "Virgin Angel: The rise and rise of Richard Branson," *Sunday Times Magazine*, May 30, 1993.
3   Kaye, Mark and Ye, Danzhao, "Behind Virgin's success: how Richard Branson motivates people," working paper.
4   Mitchell, Alan, *Leadership by Richard Branson*, Amrop International, 1995.
5   Interview in *Inc.* magazine, November 1987.
6   Jackson, Tim, *Virgin King*, HarperCollins, London, 1994.
7   Gerrard, Nicci, 'Why do we love Richard Branson?' *The Observer*, February 8, 1998.
8   Branson, Richard, "The Money Programme," BBC, July 1998.

Five

DO RIGHT BY YOUR BRAND

"I believe there is almost no limit to what a brand
can do, but only if used properly."
– Richard Branson

One of the most frequently asked questions about Virgin is how far the brand can stretch. Some commentators believe that by putting the Virgin name on such a wide range of products and services, Branson risks seriously diluting the brand.

Branson's answer to this criticism is that as long as the brand's integrity is not compromised, then it is infinitely elastic.

Just how powerful the Virgin brand is was shown by a 1997 survey. It found that 96% of British consumers have heard of Virgin and 96% can correctly name Richard Branson as its founder.

"Virgin is a unique phenomenon on the British business scene," notes one commentator. "It has, essentially, one principal asset, and an intangible one at that – its name. From financial services through airlines and railways to entertainment Megastores and soft drinks, clothes and even bridal salons, the brand is instantly recognizable to the consumer, conjuring up an image of good quality, cheap prices, and a trendy hipness that few others can match."[1]

Branson intends to keep it that way. But he acknowledges that the Virgin strategy would not work for any brand; it is based on what he calls "reputational branding" rather than traditional product and service branding.

HAVE BRAND, WILL TRAVEL

Originally aimed at younger people, today Virgin has a wider target audience. As Branson has matured so too has the brand's appeal. "Four years ago we crossed over into appealing to their parents," he says. "But we have to be careful we don't lose the kids. I'd like people to feel most of their needs in life can be filled by Virgin. The absolutely critical thing is we must never let them down."[2]

By the mid 1990s, Virgin seemed to be everywhere. So ubiquitous had the brand become that hardly a day seemed to go by without seeing a grinning Richard Branson launching some new Virgin product or service. The famous flying V logo was emblazoned on aircraft, megastore and cinema fronts, and was about to make its debut on cola cans.

The activity prompted some to question the company's strategy. Those who understood what he was about, however, recognized that what Branson had created was an entirely new kind of brand proposition. John Murphy, chairman of the famous brand consultancy Interbrand, for example, observed that: "Unless they poison someone or start applying the brand to inappropriate products such as pension funds or photocopiers, I doubt whether the Virgin brand will ever be diluted." Little did Murphy know that by 1996, Virgin Direct would be offering financial services – including pensions.

STRETCHING A POINT

Branson is critical of the traditional Western view of branding. He likens Virgin's approach to that of some Japanese companies. Referring to the decision by Mars not to use its famous brand name on pet food products, he says: "What I call 'Mars Syndrome' infects every marketing department and advertising agency in the country. They think that brands only relate to products and that there is a limited amount of stretch that is possible. They seem to have forgotten that no-one has a problem playing a Yamaha piano, having ridden a Yamaha motorbike that day, or listening to a Mitsubishi stereo in a Mitsubishi car, driving past a Mitsubishi bank."

Branson on brand stretching: "No-one has a problem playing a Yamaha piano, having ridden a Yamaha motorbike that day, or listening to a Mitsubishi stereo in a Mitsubishi car, driving past a Mitsubishi bank."

"The idea of brands crossing corporate structures and product areas ... has found its modern manifestation in the Japanese management structure 'keiretsu', where different business act as a family under one brand name."

The point for would-be brand-builders to realize is that the most important aspect of the Virgin brand proposition is its credibility among its market segment. Just as existing Virgin products and services provide credibility for new offerings, the relationship between the Virgin family could also work in reverse. If the image were to become tarnished by association with a shoddy product or poor service or an offering that was a rip-off, then the standing of the wider Virgin brand could be damaged. His foray into the UK railway market has done his brand no favors. Time will tell whether the criticism that Virgin Trains services have attracted will do lasting damage to the Virgin umbrella brand.

KEEPING THE FAITH

For all his japes, Richard Branson takes the reputation of the Virgin brand extremely seriously. "Your brand name is only as good as your reputation," he says. "Ours is of tremendous value."

What is perhaps unique about the Virgin brand is that it is, as one of the company's slogans puts it, "a lifetime relationship." Will Whitehorn, director of corporate affairs at Virgin management and long-time colleague of Branson, observes: "At Virgin we know what the brand means and when we put our brand name on something, we're making a promise. It's a promise we've always kept and always will. It's harder work keeping promises than making them, but there is no secret formula. Virgin sticks to its principles and keeps its promises."

Branson has acknowledged time and time again that the most vital asset Virgin has is its reputation. Put the Virgin name on any product that doesn't come up to scratch and the whole company is brought into disrepute. "Our customers trust us," he says.

The Branson philosophy, then, is: look after your brand and it will last. There is, however, and always has been a tension at the heart of the Virgin brand. For all his unquestioned emphasis on the integrity of the Virgin name, one of Branson's personal characteristics – that has become a strand of what Virgin stands for – is a certain restlessness. He has an insatiable desire to take risks and explore new areas. It is in his blood that Branson has to be constantly expanding the borders of the empire. Yet it is vital to do so without damaging the good name of the company. This creates something of a dilemma. It is one that Branson is well aware of.

"We are expanding and growing our use of the brand," he says, "but are always mindful of the fact that we should only put it on products and services that fit – or will fit – our very exacting criteria."

In recent years, he has thought long and hard about what the Virgin brand stands for. He believes the reputation the company has built up is based on five key factors: value for money; quality; reliability; innovation; and an indefinable, but nonetheless palpable, sense of fun. (Another, slightly snappier, version of the Virgin brand values is: genuine and fun; contemporary and different; consumers' champion; and first class at business-class price.)[3]

In a classic piece of reverse engineering, these are now the brand values that Virgin applies when considering new business ventures.

He says any new product or service must have, or have the prospect of having in the future, the following attributes:

◆ it must be of the best quality

◆ it must be innovative

◆ it must be good value for money

◆ it must be challenging to existing alternatives

◆ and it must add a sense of fun or cheekiness.

Virgin claims that many projects it considers are potentially very profitable but, if they don't fit with the Group's values, they are rejected.[4] But Branson says: "If an idea satisfies at least four of these five criteria, we'll usually take a serious look at it."

MAKING WAVES

If you've got a great brand and can see a market opportunity, you shouldn't let a little thing like whether you have any experience of that market get in the way. According to Branson: "If you know how to motivate and deal with people, it doesn't matter whether you are taking on the airline industry, the soft drinks industry or the film industry. The same rules apply."

"But you should never go into an industry just with the purpose of making money. One has to passionately believe it is possible to change the industry, to turn it on its head, to make sure that it will never be the same again. With the right people and that conviction, anything is possible. And you can then ignore those who go on about brand stretching."

Lately, however, Branson's belief that Virgin can change the way that industries are perceived has come under pressure. The company's involvement with trains – especially the investment-starved British railway network – has drawn criticism.

After initial excitement that Virgin would bring a breath of fresh air and punctuality to parts of the famously tardy British Rail network, commuters have been disappointed. Virgin services quickly gained a reputation for being both dilapidated and late. Branson explained that it would take five years to bring the service up to the standards Virgin expects. Some critics say the adventure has damaged the Virgin brand. Branson believes the company's good name is more robust than that.

"If you have 20 or 30 years of good reputation behind you, the public get to know you like you're a brother or sister," he says. "They know you and the companies' strengths – they know your weaknesses. A brand built on that length of reputation should be able to withstand the occasional slip up and even come out stronger as a result."[5]

> **Branson on brand reputation:** "If you have 20 or 30 years of good reputation behind you, the public get to know you like you're a brother or sister."

BEARD FACED CHEEK

There is one other intangible but vital ingredient to the Branson marketing mix. Whatever Virgin does, it adds a sense of fun or cheekiness. "In the early days," he says, "the actual Virgin name itself was perceived as slightly risqué. We weren't even allowed to register it for three years with the Patent office because they felt it was "rude."

"But sometimes you have to take some risk in developing a brand. EMI felt that having the Sex Pistols on their books would damage the company's reputation. We felt that it was just the ticket to take Virgin out of the hippy era and to attract more modern artists. Court cases over the name of the album *Never Mind the Bollocks, Here's the Sex Pistols* only helped strengthen Virgin's image."

And it's not just Virgin record covers that tease the establishment. Every Virgin product or service has a slightly tongue-in-cheek approach. It is not that the company goes into anything in an unprofessional way – far from it. It's simply that it has a sense of humor. Often the joke is at the expense of its venerable chairman.

Consider, for example, the advertising campaign for the company's financial services company Virgin Direct. At a time when another leading UK provider was running a campaign based around the sensible and somewhat staid image of its chief executive, Virgin offered 1960s footage of a young and geekish looking Branson, complete with Joe Ninety specs and a hair-cut from hell. The message? Presumably, that even wayward entrepreneurs have to grow up sometime.

More recently, a double page advertisement was placed in *The Times* and other leading newspapers. The full color promotion for the Virgin designer clothes label featured a grinning picture of Branson in one of his most dreadful patterned jumpers. The caption read: "Georgio designs. Ralph designs. Calvin designs. Richard doesn't."

DO RIGHT BY YOUR BRAND

One of the most frequently asked questions about Virgin is how far the brand can stretch. Branson's answer is that as long as the brand's integrity is not compromised, then it is infinitely elastic. Virgin's strategy is based on what he calls "reputational branding" rather than traditional product and service branding. Lessons from Branson the brand master are:

◆ A good brand travels. The ubiquitous Virgin brand has prompted some commentators to ask whether the brand is being diluted. Those who understood what Branson was about, however, recognize that he has created an entirely new kind of brand proposition.

◆ Brand elasticity is infinite. The most important aspect of the Virgin brand proposition is its credibility among its market segment. Existing Virgin products and services provide credibility for new offerings.

◆ Love, honor and cherish your brand. Branson has acknowledged time and time again that the most vital asset Virgin has is its reputation. His philosophy is: look after your brand and it will last.

◆ Rules are for breaking. If you've got a great brand and can see a market opportunity, you shouldn't let a little thing like whether you have any experience of that market get in the way.

◆ A pinch of salt adds flavor. Whatever Virgin does, it adds a sense of fun or cheekiness. It is not that the company goes into anything in an unprofessional way – far from it. It's simply that it has a sense of humor.

NOTES

1   Rodgers, Paul, "The Branson Phenomenon," *Enterprise* magazine, March/April 1997.
2   Rodgers, Paul, "The Branson Phenomenon," *Enterprise* magazine, March/April 1997.
3   Campbell, Andrew and Sadtler, David, "Corporate Break-ups," *Strategy & Business*, Third Quarter 1998.
4   Virgin Group literature.
5   Branson, Richard, "Money Programme" lecture, BBC, July 1998.

Six

SMILE FOR THE CAMERAS

"There are some who believe that in his own charm-ingly haphazard way, Branson runs the slickest public relations operation in Britain."
– Andrew Davidson, journalist

He may not look like a finely tuned PR machine, but Richard Branson has turned himself into a walking, talking logo. Where McDonald's has the red haired clown Ronald McDonald, and Disney has a six foot mouse; Virgin has its goofy chairman. Every time his picture appears in a newspaper or magazine, it promotes the Virgin brand.

This is entirely deliberate, and probably one of the most effective promotional strategies ever employed by a company. The risk to the reputation of the brand, of course, is correspondingly high should Branson's personal image become tarnished. To date, however,[1] it has proved highly successful, enabling him to build the Virgin brand on a shoestring advertising budget.

Calculating the advertising value of Branson's failed attempt to circumnavigate the globe in a hot air balloon, one American advertising executive said "there aren't enough zeros to do the maths."

It is his ability to orchestrate publicity for his business venture which, perhaps more than any other facet, singles out Richard Branson from every other business leader. Even the likes of Anita Roddick, Bill Gates and Ted Turner don't generate positive coverage like Branson. Public relations is Branson's special gift.

As Tim Jackson, author of *Virgin King*, observes: "Achieving good press has been as important in Branson's business career as making sure the books balance at the end of the year. From his first days as a magazine publisher and record retailer, Branson knew that descriptions of his ventures as successful and expansionary could become self-fulfilling."

> "From his first days as a magazine publisher and record retailer, Branson knew that descriptions of his ventures as successful and expansionary could become self-fulfilling."

But with the launch of Virgin Atlantic Airways he learned a new trick. The big airlines spend literally millions of dollars on advertising every year. Branson soon realized that free media coverage was the only way he could hope to survive. This gave rise to a series of daredevil escapades and publicity stunts. Apparently, the decision to challenge for the Blue Riband – attempting to break the record for the fastest Atlantic crossing – was made when Branson discovered he couldn't afford New York TV advertising rates to promote his airline.

It is a tactic that Branson has used to remarkable effect ever since, setting aside about a quarter of his time for PR activities.[2]

HOLD THE FRONT PAGE

Where other companies spend huge sums of money on advertising, Branson generates yards of column inches for free. And

where other firms employ expensive PR firms to organize contrived media events, Branson delivers a much more valuable
commodity – news.

The secret to his self-serving publicity campaigns is an instinctive understanding of what appeals to the media. To publicize
the launch of his airline, for example, Branson arrived at the
inaugural press conference wearing a brown leather aviator's
helmet, Biggles style. Editors loved it, and splashed Branson's
photograph all over their newspapers. The story generated so
much public interest that Virgin didn't need to advertise its
first flights.

Since then Branson's media events have escalated. To launch
Virgin Cola in the US, for instance, he drove a full battle tank
down a busy New York City street to demolish a wall of cola
cans. No surprises for guessing which company made the news
the next day.

But his eye-catching performances and dazzling timing actually mask a self-conscious streak. In the early days, Branson
went out of his way to avoid interviews with journalists. To those
who have not met him, the idea that Branson might be shy
seems ridiculous. Closer observation reveals that although he
is an exhibitionist in some regards, he can also appear diffi-
dent and awkward. There is, in fact, something of the actor
about him. In front of the cameras, he looks like a man performing a role that has been written for him. Branson himself
acknowledges as much, and insists that he has to force himself
to perform.

"Up to the time I launched the airline, I was a reasonably shy person. I didn't like doing interviews, avoided the press. I took my mother's advice to let my businesses speak for themselves. But when we decided to launch an airline, Freddie Laker said that if I was going to take on American Airlines, United and British Airways, I would never have the advertising spend that they employ ... but if I went and made a bit of a fool of myself, I'd get on the front covers."[3]

Where other tycoons appear pompous and self important, Branson radiates schoolboy enthusiasm.

His shyness actually adds to his appeal. Where other tycoons appear pompous and self important, Branson radiates schoolboy enthusiasm. The fact that his public persona is self created and goes against the grain makes it all the more impressive. He is a self-made media icon.

What is beyond doubt is that Branson's feel for public relations is a gift. His instinctive ability to recognize and exploit a media opportunity allows him to run rings around the staid and conservative businessmen the public are used to seeing. Contrived or not, Branson manages to appear "natural" and even "spontaneous" even when you know he has been answering the same questions all day.

His instincts allow him to avoid the clichés of PR that most self-publicists eventually fall into. His slightly awkward delivery, packed with umms and ahs, sounds unscripted. There is a frankness about Branson, too, that is endearing. What he has that others lack is credibility – something that he retains even when he is involved in a blatant PR exercise.

Asked if Virgin's high proportion of Black and Asian employees is the result of a conscious non-discrimination policy, he replies: "Perhaps it should be, but it just happened that way." Told of a press report that denied his companies were registered offshore to avoid British tax, he responds: "It's wrong. The decision was tax led."

No amount of pre-interview briefing could provide such a smooth passage through potential media minefields.

At times, the drama has been all too real. When his attempt to circumnavigate the globe in the hot air balloon went dangerously wrong, with the *Global Challenger* falling at a rate of 2000 feet per minute, no one was in any doubt that the lives of the crew – Branson among them – were in serious danger. As the drama unfolded, Alex Ritchie, the 52-year-old senior engineer on the project and a last minute stand-in for the third crew member, made a heroic climb onto the balloon to release additional weight, averting disaster. The record attempt had failed, but commercially it was a triumph.

It had cost £3 million for the Global Challenger to travel barely 400 miles. But no one from the world of marketing was in any doubt that it had been money well spent. Referring to a £300 million Pepsi Co. advertising campaign that included repainting Concorde blue, one British PR expert claimed that simply by leaving the ground, Branson had "outdone Pepsi fourfold."[4]

One anecdote highlights his aptitude for media relations. On his second and successful attempt to bring back the Blue Riband to Britain for the fastest sea crossing of the Atlantic, Virgin staff back on dry land were kept busy throughout much of the voyage going through a list of the UK's national and regional media. From the operational headquarters in one of Virgin's record stores, they called the editors one by one and offered to patch them through for a live interview with Branson on board the Virgin Atlantic Challenger II.

While Branson answered questions from one newspaper, the next would be receiving a background briefing from the land-based staff and waiting to be put through. The Challenger's skipper kept this up for hours, answering the same questions and making the same wise cracks again and again to obtain maximum coverage. Finally, he turned to Chay Blyth, the round-the-world yachtsman accompanying him on the record attempt, and said: "This is getting boring. We've got to tell them something else." "We've just missed a whale," the astute yachtsman said by way of reply. "Where, where?," asked Branson getting excited. "I didn't see it." It was only when he glanced back at Blyth that he realized that, whale or no whale, the story made good newspaper copy. "Oh yeah," he said, "I've got it." The next few editors heard about the huge sea creature that had had such a close brush with the boat. Naturally, they lapped it up.

So well known is Branson's talent for a good story that new Virgin ventures have little difficulty now in arousing public and media interest. Virgin Bride, the company's chain of bridal stores, was still 18 months off launch when a rumor, started in a West London estate agent, reached all the national newspapers within three days. The company even received a phone call from the *Los Angeles Times*.[5]

ALL TEETH AND NO TROUSERS

Branson will do almost anything to promote his brand. This is complemented by his yen for adventure. His headline-grabbing activities include daredevil attempts to become the first person to circumnavigate the globe in a hot air balloon, which very nearly cost him his life, and setting a new world speed record for crossing the Atlantic in a speedboat. Such exploits resonate with the message "life is an adventure; life is fun" – which matches the Virgin approach to business.

The Virgin chairman is especially good at creating stories with visual impact. He is prepared to dress up and act the clown, where most businessmen take themselves far too seriously to do any such thing. Certainly most chairmen of large companies draw the line at wearing fancy dress costumes to promote their products. In the public's mind, of course, Branson's willingness to play the fool only serves to emphasize what a bunch of stuffed shirts the others are.

"I've worn almost every costume there is to wear," says Branson. "It makes a back-page photo into a front-page one. And they come back for more."

An even more outrageous Branson ploy is cross-dressing. This he used to good effect when launching his new airline – he donned stewardess uniform – and more recently when he modeled a wedding dress and high heels for the launch of his new chain of bridal stores. How many other company chairmen would dress up in women's underwear – in public?

Branson on fancy dress:

"I've worn almost every costume there is to wear. It makes a back-page photo into a front-page one."

In fact, among Virgin staff the chairman's exhibitionist tendencies are well known. He seems to have a passion for dressing up and stripping off in equal measure. One senior employee[6] recalls that Branson's propensity to strip off reached the point where a groan went up on one trip to Switzerland when he offered to bet everyone £10 that he would dare to ski all the way downhill stark naked. Nobody took him up on the bet, but Branson went through with the dare anyway.

The *Sun* newspaper once reported that on a Virgin weekend away, he had entertained employees at a seafood restaurant by performing a table top striptease in fishnet stockings and lacy suspenders. The story ran under the headline: "Shocking stockings caper by pop tycoon."

The newspaper even managed to get hold of a photograph of the incident, in which Branson was instantly recognizable by his trademark – the brightly patterned sweater he was wearing.

At the time, Virgin was a listed company on the London Stock Exchange. Such a story might have damaged the company's share price. Indeed, in the same year, reports that Ralph Halpern, the 48-year-old chairman of the men's wear retailer the Burton Group, had had an affair with a 19-year-old topless model, were followed by a drop in the company's share price.

But the *Sun* article was actually favorable. It praised the Virgin chairman for his "down to earth" attitude and a sense of fun which, it quipped in true *Sun* style, was "Virgin on the ridiculous." The one note of criticism came from claims that the weekend had cost the company £250,000 (the company said the real cost was closer to half that figure).

Virgin investors seemed to take Branson's behavior as only to be expected from a someone who hobnobbed with pop stars and hippies, ran his company from a boat, and refused to wear a suit.

BRANSON: SUPER HERO

Branson also has a remarkable knack of popping up at unexpected moments of public drama. In the run-up to the Gulf War, for example, when a British Airways plane and crew was held hostage by Saddam Hussein's forces, Branson informed the British media that he had offered Prime Minister John Major the use of a Virgin aircraft to get them out. He put a plane on 24-hour standby to fly in and bring the hostages home.

Just days after Princess Diana announced that she would be withdrawing from public life because of media pressure, she appeared on the same platform as Branson to launch a new addition to the Virgin Atlantic fleet. Diana looked relaxed and at ease as Branson sprayed her with champagne and persuaded her to pose in a red Virgin Atlantic jacket. (PR genius is not too strong a term for Branson.)

When the pop star Boy George found himself in difficult straits over his heroin addiction, who stepped in to offer a fatherly hand of help? None other than Richard Branson, whose Virgin record label had discovered George in his Culture Club days. Branson whisked the troubled pop star away from the media gaze and checked him into a top drug rehabilitation clinic. Cynics saw a blatant PR opportunist at work, but others saw the Virgin boss as the caring face of the pop business.

PHILANTHROPY AND STAMP COLLECTING ARE TWO DIFFERENT THINGS

There is also another aspect to Richard Branson that receives media attention. Over the years, he has been involved in a number of high-profile community activities. These include two unsuccessful bids to run Britain's National Lottery – with all profits to go to a charitable foundation; his involvement in the Aids awareness campaign – which gave rise to the launch of Mates condoms to challenge the near monopoly position of Durex in the UK market and from which all profits go to charity; his support for a non-smoking campaign aimed at children;

and his involvement in the UK government sponsored UK 2000 initiative to help unemployed youngsters and clean up the litter from Britain's streets.

There has even been talk of Branson taking on a major public office, with rumors that he would enter the race for the new post of Mayor of London. It is a testament to his public popularity, too, that polls indicated that he would have been the first choice of many Londoners.

These "public spirited" activities reveal Branson the philanthropist. Although they are generally separate from his business empire, they also generate publicity for the Virgin group. This has prompted some people to question Branson's motives.

Many celebrities, of course, are well known for their less-than-charitable reasons for taking on charitable works. Film stars, pop stars and politicians are not above milking sentiment from the odd good cause for a bit of popular press. In Branson's case, however, such accusations seem misplaced. Certainly, his personal reputation has benefited from championing worthy causes, but his reasons, in the main, seem to be genuinely idealistic. This is the man, after all, who at the age of 18 founded the non-profit Student Advisory Centre to help with young people's problems. That was back in 1968, before he'd even started the mail-order record business that laid the seeds for the Virgin empire.

In fact, if there is one area where Richard Branson has not received the credit he is due, it is his charitable work. For such an enthusiastic and able self-publicist, he has shown himself to be uncharacteristically clumsy when it comes to obtaining positive coverage for his good works. Although he does not give vast amounts of money to charity, Branson has given generously of his energy and time to support causes he believes in. He has been involved in three major public projects.

The first was the UK 2000 campaign, an initiative to pool the resources of a number of private and government schemes to improve Britain's environment and provide meaningful work experience for unemployed youngsters. At the request of Margaret Thatcher's government, Branson accepted the role of chairman. From the very outset, however, the campaign was plagued by hostile press coverage, with the British tabloids determined to portray it as no more than an exercise in picking up litter. Branson left the post a year later, licking his wounds.

His second public spirited foray involved the launch of Mates, a brand of cut-price condoms aimed at shaking up the near monopoly position of Durex. The launch of Mates was a business success, putting condom advertisements on British television for the first time. But, despite raising public awareness of HIV, the advertising had little real impact on public health, which was its stated aim. Branson was criticized by the press even though he risked his own money to launch a product whose proceeds were intended for charity.

Branson's bid for the UK National Lottery franchise also earned him unfavorable press coverage. Despite his insistence that he would make no profits from running the lottery and that all of the proceeds would be administered by a charitable foundation entirely separate from the Virgin group, Branson failed to get his message across to the public. Once again, cynical journalists played fast and loose with his altruistic intentions.

It is an interesting insight into Branson's personality, too, that he appears to be surprisingly sensitive to such criticism. Where most people in the public eye would expect to be misunderstood, Branson appears almost naïve about why the press might pick on him. Indeed, he seems genuinely disappointed that journalists should question the motivation behind his public-spirited displays. Perhaps he has just become used to positive coverage. Alternatively, he may see playing the hurt party as the best way to deflect criticism.

NOW YOU SEE ME, NOW YOU DON'T

Almost as impressive as his ability to steal the limelight when he wants to is the Virgin chairman's ability to avoid negative publicity for his business activities or have his private life reported by the media. Like the Cheshire Cat in *Alice in Wonderland*, Branson seems to be able to vanish when it suits him, so that all that remains visible is his toothy smile.

While others with alternative business credos such as Anita Roddick have been punished by the press if they put a foot wrong, many of Branson's business setbacks and failures remain discretely hidden from the public gaze. Roddick, it seems, is penalized for her apparent self-righteousness and for taking what some see as a marketing gimmick too seriously. Branson, on the other hand, is seen as a schoolboy prankster and given the benefit of the doubt. This may explain why when Branson has received critical press coverage it has tended to be for his philanthropic activities rather than his commercial adventures.

By and large, the media attention Virgin receives is positive. The other side of the Branson media manipulation is his ability to drop out of sight when it suits him. From time to time there are rumors of cash shortages within the Virgin Group, and that he has overstretched himself. The fact that his business is a private company with most of its interests registered through offshore trusts makes it very difficult for outsiders to know what the true balance sheet position is. This perfectly legal and tax-efficient arrangement works to Branson's advantage.

Branson has managed to keep a veil around the inner workings of his financial empire. In 1986 he floated his Virgin business on the London Stock Exchange, only to buy it back because he didn't like the constraints a market listing brought with it.

It has been suggested that there are two Richard Bransons: the people's champion known to millions and the deal maker known to his business partners.

His ability to step out of the limelight and virtually disappear from view is both part of the secret of his enduring success, and also part of the way in which he protects his business interests from damaging speculation. Nor will you see his children in the media spotlight – his wife Joan sees to that. How Branson achieves this remarkable conjuring trick is unclear. Perhaps it is part of the art of being an everyman character to be able to disappear into the woodwork when it suits. Having a Caribbean island of your own to disappear to and throwing excellent parties for the media probably help, too.

SMILE FOR THE CAMERAS

He may not look like a finely tuned PR machine, but Richard Branson has turned himself into a walking, talking logo. Every time his picture appears in a newspaper or magazine, it promotes the Virgin brand. Promoting your business the Branson way has a number of subtle and not-so-subtle twists to it. These include:

◆ Understand what the media want, and give it to them. Where other companies spend huge sums of money on advertising, Branson generates yards of column inches for free. And where other firms employ expensive PR firms to organize contrived media events, Branson delivers a much more valuable commodity – news.

◆ Think in pictures. Branson will do almost anything to promote his brand. He is especially good at creating stories with visual impact.

◆ Stand up and be counted. Branson has a remarkable knack of popping up at unexpected moments of public drama.

◆ Remember, philanthropy and stamp collecting are two different things. Over the years, Branson has been involved in a number of high-profile community activities. Although these are generally separate from his business empire, they also generate publicity for the Virgin group.

◆ Know when to duck. Almost as impressive as Branson's ability to steal the limelight when he wants to is his ability to avoid negative publicity for his business activities.

NOTES

1   And despite an allegation of sexual harassment.
2   Mitchell, Alan, *Leadership by Richard Branson*, Amrop International, 1995.
3   "I'm Richard, fly me," Roy Hattersley, *The Guardian*, June 20, 1998.
4   Brown, Mick, *Richard Branson: The Authorized Biography*, 4th edn, Headline, 1998.
5   Virgin Group Literature.
6   Jackson, Tim, *Virgin King*, HarperCollins, London, 1994, p. 126.

Seven

DON'T LEAD SHEEP, HERD CATS

"Virgin staff are not mere hired hands. They are not managerial pawns in some gigantic chess game. They are entrepreneurs in their own right."[1]
– Richard Branson

Don't lead sheep; herd cats – that's the Branson style of leadership. Rather than expect people to follow blindly where he leads, he relies on his ability to get the best from individuals by creating a challenging environment. Like herding cats, it's much harder to do but a lot more lively.

In many ways, the Virgin boss is the archetypal leader of the future. He rarely coerces, inspiring instead. He possesses that most precious of all leadership assets – credibility. You could say he obtains the best performance from the people around him not through threats but through pure adulation. Alternatively, he is a just a fairly talented entrepreneur carried along by his own enthusiasm and a long run of luck. Unlikely. In reality, it is because he doesn't "play" the big leader like an actor, but works hard at it, that he is so effective in the role. What Branson understands better than most is that leadership is an art: but one that is more akin to the skill of the orchestra conductor than the soloist.

> What Branson understands better than most is that leadership is an art: but one that is more akin to the skill of the orchestra conductor than the soloist.

Leadership is, perhaps, the most difficult of all human attributes to define. In terms of style of leadership, there is much to be said for timing. Cometh the hour, as they say, cometh the man. Whatever else we think about the business leaders of the 21st century, it seems clear that in terms of style they will be more Branson than Lord Hanson. The days of the asset strippers are numbered. The ability to manage start-ups and put empires together is more valued than that of selling off the family silver.

But all the style in the world cannot compensate for a lack of substance. Perhaps that is why inadequate business leaders prefer to hide behind their job titles and status symbols, relying on hierarchical power for their authority. Successful entrepreneurs, on the other hand, have tended to be figures of awe; inspiring fear and wonder in equal measure.

Today, we are less impressed with either of these styles. The modern view is that leadership relies on people being willing to follow. When Richard Branson started out in business back in the 1960s there was little to suggest that command and control was crumbling, certainly not in the corporate world. By discarding hierarchical power in favor of inspirational leadership, Branson was 25 years ahead of his time.

LEADING FROM THE REAR

One of the characteristics of the Branson leadership style is knowing when to get out the way and let people get on with it. The way that Virgin is structured means he really has no choice. With up to 200 companies in the Virgin family, it simply isn't feasible to think he could be hands-on boss of all of them. Whether by luck or design, then, Branson is forced to be a back-seat leader. (The one company that he doesn't seem able to leave alone is Virgin Atlantic.)

By and large, though, the hands-off leadership style is highly beneficial. Managers in the group enjoy the opportunity of running their own show; they find it highly motivating. Unlike most companies, too, they don't waste time on unnecessary meetings and pointless reports to give corporate headquarters something to do. This is because there are fewer than 25 people based in the Virgin head office, including Branson himself.

So if he isn't running the business on a day-to-day basis what does Virgin's back seat leader actually do? It's hard to describe exactly. You could say, he enthuses other people, contributing to the buzz that emanates from every part of the group.

Beyond that, Branson is also important as a figurehead for the Virgin brand. He puts his full support behind new ventures. The publicity he generates, promotes all of the companies in the group. These days, he has to ration his personal appearances to one or two media events per business per year.

But there is something more to the Branson leadership model. He stands for something that makes people feel good to work for his company, a set of values that are important to Virgin employees. It's hard to pin down exactly what those values are, but they have something to do with running a business for a purpose other than purely profit.

CATALYTIC CONVERTER

Another vital aspect of Branson's role as "leader" of Virgin is that of planning the future. Unlike business visionaries such as Microsoft's Bill Gates, and Intel's Andy Grove, however, he is not in the business of crystal ball gazing or strategizing. Rather, Branson is a prospector, panning the multitude of business ideas that Virgin attracts for nuggets of purest gold.

He is always on the lookout for new business ventures. He and his two expert advisers consider somewhere close to 50 proposals a week. Most will be rejected out of hand, but if there is a gleam of an opportunity for a new Virgin company they will take a long hard look.

It is one thing to recognize potential for a business, and quite another thing to make it a reality. This is one of Branson's secrets: the ability to make things happen. He is the catalyst that triggers a chain reaction that transforms potential energy in a project or idea into kinetic energy that sends people scurrying in a thousand directions.

When the business consultant Don Cruickshank was brought in as group managing director to prepare Virgin for privatization, he quickly realized that trying to get Branson to fit into a conventional organizational structure was pointless – and would be self-defeating. Instead, he sensibly concluded, the company would have to be structured around its energetic chairman.

Recognizing his talent for enthusing others, Cruickshank, the ex-McKinsey consultant, encouraged Branson to "continue to dream up new ideas, to look at a bewildering array of new ventures and to start more companies in two years than most entrepreneurs do in their whole careers."[2]

Branson should not try to alter his nature, Cruickshank warned. Instead he should stick to what he is really good at: motivating others and passing on his confidence and belief that every new project would succeed. In short, Branson should devote all his energy to acting as a catalyst. All that was needed was a corps of people to tidy up behind him, and to help him clarify what he was trying to achieve.

One of Branson's great talents is getting people fired up about a new business idea and then letting them loose on it. His own enthusiasm is contagious, focusing excitement on a goal or destination which then allows him to step back and let others run with it. Somehow, too, he spurs people on to achievements they wouldn't have believed were possible.

TALENT SCOUT

When you get right down to it, Richard Branson has no clearly defined business skill or training. He's not really a numbers man – he failed his elementary maths examination three times. Nor is he an IT whiz-kid – he doesn't know how to switch on a lap top, let alone design an operating system. Marketing and publicity he has a flair for but little grasp of or interest in the theory, preferring to do it his way. What then does Branson bring to the party? (Apart from the party itself.)

Branson on his staff: "Virgin staff are not mere hired hands. They are not managerial pawns in some gigantic chess game. They are entrepreneurs in their own right."

"What I do best is finding people and letting them work," he says. "Virgin staff are not mere hired hands. They are not managerial pawns in some

gigantic chess game. They are entrepreneurs in their own
right."[3]

It seems that what Branson is good at is surrounding himself
with very talented people and creating the right environment
for them to flourish. This is no mean feat.

Over the years, Branson's personal reputation has proved one
of the most effective ways of recruiting staff. A great many of
Virgin's most able managers actually approached Branson,
drawn by what they had seen and heard about the way he runs
his business. One of his great contributions to the business is
to act as a magnet for these people, and to recognize and reward them when they appear. He is a talent scout.

The same principle applies to business opportunities. These
days Branson spends much of his time reviewing the many
business proposals made to Virgin by other companies. Good
prospects are those that involve institutionalized markets, fit
the Virgin brand (genuine and fun; contemporary and different; consumers' champion; and first class at business-class
prices), will respond to the Virgin recipe, offering an enticing
risk-to-reward ratio and are presented by a capable management team.

Where Virgin ventures have not been successful, it has been
noted,[4] it is often when he has had a good idea himself and
gone out to look for a manager to run it. The best business
proposals have come to him from managers who want to run
the business themselves. He is better at spotting talent when it
comes to him than he is at going out and finding it.

MASTER OF MAYHEM

Branson's other great leadership role is to preside over and encourage the creative environment that gives Virgin its special buzz. "A mad house," is how one visitor described the group's premises. "There were people running about all over the place."

Another described the scene at Albion Street, the site of Branson's first business venture, in 1969: "Phones were ringing; attractive women were coming and going. At the other end of the room, a young man with tousled light brown hair and a dazzling smile was talking very earnestly into the telephone."

Yet another described the Virgin headquarters in Holland Park: "There are dirty plates stacked up in the kitchen above Richard Branson's office. There is a photocopier on the landing. All over the house where he oversees his 200 companies there are doors ajar, mugs left on tables, people wandering in and out … it is nothing like a modern corporate headquarters."[5]

And in the centre of all the mayhem, there is always Richard Branson: usually working the telephone, charming, teasing, cajoling, shouting, or in some other way trying to get someone to do something to the benefit of Virgin.

Like the director of a Marx Brothers film, Branson is the master of mayhem, orchestrating the chaos. In his own opinion, he does so with commendable restraint, leaving the managers of the Virgin companies to make their own decisions and seldom interfering in operational matters.

"The bosses of each company have almost total authority to make their own decisions. If I do make a suggestion, quite often they tell me to fuck off," he says.

But there is another view. The reason Virgin never worked as a public company, his critics say, is because Branson is a control freak who hates to be accountable to anyone. He is also, say the critics, an inveterate meddler, who undermines the authority of his managers by interfering in decisions that he has supposedly delegated.

"The 'hippy capitalist' has become a business visionary whose management style and philosophy offers some potentially crucial lessons for capitalism in the throes of change."

Contrary to Branson's own claims, says one disgruntled former employee, the Virgin top management "all sit there like nodding dogs, their heads nodding whichever way Branson's does. None of his management dare go to the toilet without asking him first."

These and other accusations have been leveled at Branson, but it is difficult to see how such pandemonium could be ruled over by such a panjandrum. Most dictators rely on rules to keep people in line. Branson's empire is closer to chaos.

SHIP AHOY

Branson has been called a visionary, a sage, a guru even. "The 'hippy capitalist' has become a business visionary whose management style and philosophy offers some potentially crucial lessons for capitalism in the throes of change," notes one commentator.[6]

"A child of the revolutionary 1960s, he's forged a unique synthesis of the youth revolution's values and the needs of a modern business ... somehow his values and style allay our nagging doubts about the morality of modern capitalism's ends and means."

Utopian in the romantic sense he may be, but Branson is no social engineer. He has no blueprint. Even if he thought he knew the answer, Branson wouldn't want to alienate people from the Virgin brand by explaining it.

Although he has an outrageous sense of humor, he is far too politically correct to offend any particular social group. When asked questions on controversial topics his typical response is to offer multiple choice answers, indicating there are many dimensions to the issue, or to suggest that perhaps "there is no right or wrong answer."

In truth, the "vision thing" isn't really Branson's thing. What he is good at is keeping his one good pirate's eye pressed to the telescope and constantly scanning the horizon for heavily laden treasure ships ripe for boarding. The other eye he uses to keep a watchful vigil on the here and now, and to ensure he knows what is going on with his constituency – the Virgin faithful.

One of the lessons to be learned from Branson is not to get too hung up on grandiose ideas and projects, but to move with the times. His great skill is the ability to stay in touch with Virgin's customers and employees and use that knowledge to spy new business opportunities that are ripe for the Virgin formula. As for his philosophy and ideas of a better world, it is hard to separate them from his instinctive feel for what motivates and inspires people. In other words, don't ask Branson for answers, just follow where his instinct leads.

DON'T LEAD SHEEP, HERD CATS

Rather than expect people to follow blindly where he leads, Branson relies on his ability to get the best from individuals by creating a challenging environment. Like herding cats, it's much harder to do but a lot more lively. The lessons for leaders are:

◆ Be a back seat leader. One of the characteristics of the Branson leadership style is knowing when to get out the way and let people get on with it.

◆ Act as a catalyst. Branson is the catalyst that transforms potential energy in a project or idea into kinetic energy that sends people scurrying in a thousand directions.

◆ Surround yourself with talented people. What Branson is good at is surrounding himself with very talented people and creating the right environment for them to flourish. This is no mean feat.

◆ Encourage chaos. Branson is the master of mayhem, orchestrating the chaos.

◆ Constantly scan the horizon for new opportunities. Branson's great skill is the ability to stay in touch with Virgin's customers and employees and use that knowledge to spy new business opportunities that are ripe for the Virgin formula.

NOTES

1   Mitchell, Alan, *Leadership by Richard Branson*, Amrop International, 1995.
2   Jackson, Tim, *Virgin King*, HarperCollins, London, 1994.
3   Mitchell, Alan, *Leadership by Richard Branson*, Amrop International, 1995.
4   Campbell, Andrew and Sadtler, David, "Corporate Breakups," *Strategy & Business*, Third Quarter 1998.
5   "Has he won the lottery?," *The Independent*, December 17, 1995.
6   Mitchell, Alan, *Leadership by Richard Branson*, Amrop International, 1995.

Eight

MOVE FASTER THAN A SPEEDING BULLET

"He just says Yes or No. He doesn't spend valuable time farting about trying to convince a bunch of middle managers it's a good idea."
– Rowan Gormley, CEO, Virgin Direct

If there is one area where Richard Branson's disdain for the "suits" of the corporate world is entirely justified, it is in the speed of their reactions. Management gurus are agog at the notion of a large corporation that can move quickly. In most multinationals, bureaucracy heaped on bureaucracy has created an environment where management books such as *Teaching the Elephant to Dance* and *When Giants Learn to Dance* are bestsellers.

Even the "downsizing" of recent years has failed to get to the real problem. At the heart of most companies there is a fatty layer of inefficient senior management, who couldn't make a decision if their lives depended on it. Yet, for three decades, Branson has shown his lumbering rivals the meaning of agility. Time and time again, Virgin has demonstrated how to exploit a window of opportunity.

To do so Branson relies on instinct as much as analysis. He has created exceptionally short decision-making chains. The normal committee stages are almost entirely absent.

TURBO BRANSON

Like Superman, Branson moves faster than a speeding bullet when an opportunity presents itself. There are invaluable lessons for the would-be entrepreneur of the future. An in-built supercharger can work wonders. The speed at which Branson expects to move, for example, is often breathtaking.

Virgin Atlantic Airways was literally airborne just five months after Branson first discussed the idea. Virgin Trading, the consumer goods company, was created just days before Virgin Cola was launched.

Virgin Direct, the financial services arm, was up and running in five months. "Most people would have taken two years at least," says its managing director Rowan Gormley. "Branson has fantastically good marketing instincts and he believes in them. He just says Yes or No. He doesn't spend valuable time farting about trying to convince a bunch of middle managers it's a good idea."

"He seems to work about 35 hours a day," says one long-standing Virgin employee – and he expects his staff to do the same, often placing impossible demands on their time and patience.

On many occasions Branson has used speed to outflank competitors. In one case, for example, he went to visit Ariola, the French arm of a German recording company that also handled record distribution for other companies including, at that time, Virgin. An executive let slip that Ariola planned to sign a talented singer called Julien Clerc. Branson rushed off to the bathroom and wrote down the name on his hand. As soon as the chance presented itself, he called one of the directors of Virgin's own French operations and asked him about the singer. Clerc was very popular, he was told. Branson then tracked down the singer's manager and signed Clerc to Virgin.[1]

LEAP BEFORE YOU LOOK

Branson is not a great believer in market research, preferring to trust his instinctive feel for what consumers want, often based on his own conversations with them. Where Virgin has benefited from market research it has often been carried out by a joint venture partner either prior to making a business proposition or to refine the product offering once Virgin is on board. One of the great advantages of owning such a powerful brand is that partners will often make the running.

> One of the great advantages of owning such a powerful brand is that partners will often make the running.

Once the idea has a green light from Branson, then the finer details can be honed by others. Branson's willingness to leap before he looks has important advantages. It means that Virgin can often launch new products – even whole new companies – into the marketplace much quicker than its lumbering rivals. With the speed at which the business environment changes these days, this can make all the difference between taking advantage of a window of opportunity and missing out. At the end of the day, as long as the Virgin reputation is not compromised in any way, then an unprofitable venture can be closed down.

It may sound like a cavalier attitude towards the priceless Virgin brand. However, there are a number of safeguards built into the process that allow Branson to be commercially promiscuous. It has been said that he is a bit of a control freak when it comes to joint ventures. The only partnerships with other companies that he is truly comfortable with are those where he has a controlling stake. When the Virgin name is used on another company's product, Branson retains the role of brand guardian.

"We are careful not to associate ourselves with products we cannot be proud of," he says. "And we have the right to withdraw the name at a week's notice if we are not happy with the objectives of the other company."

At the same time, in the majority of its partnerships, Virgin aims to negotiate a "super majority," with a controlling stake far in excess of the equity it has invested.

"Branson has taken a smart route for a private company," says one investment expert, "expanding through joint ventures, with outsiders putting up as much cash as possible, rather than getting in hock with banks."

THE DECISIVE MOMENT

Timing is all important to Branson's success. He is a master of the decisive moment. This is the all-important moment when an opportunity presents itself. It could be the point at which power shifts from one side to the other in a business deal; or it could be when a rival makes a fatal mistake. It may last months or just seconds, but Branson is brilliant at recognizing it and exploiting it.

In the case of British Airways and the dirty tricks affair, the decisive moment came when BA's media machine suggested that Branson's motives for making allegations against BA were to "create publicity for his airline." That mistake gave Branson's lawyers what they needed to file a libel writ against BA and its chairman Lord King. Up until that point, Virgin could do little to protect itself except try to draw media attention to what was happening. In reality, however, the allegations were too complex for the public to grasp easily. But once the decisive moment was reached, the tide turned.

Branson has also used this skill to great effect during negotiations throughout his business career, seizing on opportunities to renegotiate more favorable terms or press home some new advantage.

Timing is also absolutely critical to many of his PR activities. As in the other areas of his business life, Branson is a brilliant opportunist when it comes to the media. When it became tangled in its own sophistry about being a global airline and decided to drop the British flag from its livery, BA offered Branson a news story on a plate. Hardly was the paint dry on the BA aircraft than Branson the patriot was ordering that the union flag be included on the Virgin livery, telling journalists that if BA didn't want to fly the flag, Virgin would be proud to.

WITH A LITTLE HELP FROM MY FRIENDS

Something Branson is especially good at is persuading others to get involved in his projects. Whether it's Virgin employees or partner organizations, Branson's enthusiasm is infectious. In recent years, too, the credibility of the Virgin brand means that he has become a magnet for business proposals from other organizations.

Virgin Cola, for example, grew out of the development of a premium cola formula from a company called Cotts Europe that supplies many of the supermarkets with own brand colas. When Virgin moved into computers it was in partnership with ICL. When it went into the US retailing market it was with Blockbuster. Virgin vodka is produced by the long-established distiller William Grant. The original backroom expertise for Virgin Direct, Branson's financial services operation, came from Norwich Union, a leading UK insurance company, and subsequently from Australian Mutual Provincial (AMP).

This partly explains the speed with which Virgin companies have been set up. The huge advantage of a partner that already knows the business is that learning curves are far less steep, and specialist expertise is on tap. Once the product or service has been decided – usually a single offering to begin with – the main focus of the effort goes into getting the message right for consumers, and adding that all important cheeky Virgin twist.

The appeal of the Virgin brand name is also such that in recent years Branson has been able to take risks with other people's money as well as, and sometimes instead of, his own. But, as a story from his childhood illustrates, he has always understood the benefits of using other people's assets to resource his adventures.

The friendship between Branson and his school friend and long-time business partner Nik Powell assumed a recurring pattern. On one occasion, it was decided to "christen" Nik's new bicycle by taking it in turns to ride hell for leather down a hill towards a nearby river. The object of the game was to see who could get the closest to the edge without going in. Young Nik skidded to a halt a few feet short of the river. Then came Richard's turn. With a whoop of delight, he set off down the hill and straight into the river. Nik had to fish him out with a piece of wood. The bicycle, however, was never seen again, and Branson's parents had to find the cost of a replacement.[2]

VIRGIN'S SAMPLE OF ONE

Branson gets fired up by new ideas and converts them into business opportunities with head-spinning speed. The downside for Virgin employees is that their illustrious leader is constantly switching from one hobby horse to the next.

> "Richard Branson has the concentration of a gnat."

"Richard Branson has the concentration of a gnat," says one Virgin employee. Referring to Branson's belief that he can spot a business winner without market research, members of staff talk about VSO – Virgin's Sample of One, short hand for Branson's latest hare-brained scheme that's probably doomed to failure.

Inevitably, some of Branson's schemes have crashed spectacularly. Vanson, for example, the property business he started in 1983 cost him £12 million through its misguided investments; *Event*, a magazine he started in 1981, was a non-event.

But Branson takes such setbacks in his stride. To him, they are part of being an entrepreneur. A Branson view of the world is that "he who never made a mistake, never made anything."

Branson on taking risks:
"One should just get on with it and learn from mistakes."

According to an advertising executive who knows him well, Branson has killed off well over 100 companies. His attitude is go out and test something. You only learn by testing. Branson himself puts it more positively: "One should just get on with it and learn from mistakes," he says. "I love what I do because every single day I'm learning something new."

MOVE FASTER THAN A SPEEDING BULLET

If there is one area where Richard Branson's disdain for the "suits" of the corporate world is entirely justified, it is in the speed of their reactions. Management gurus are agog at the notion of a large corporation that can move quickly. He has created exceptionally short decision-making chains. The normal committee stages are almost entirely absent. The lessons are:

◆ Avoid paralysis by analysis. The speed at which Branson expects to move is often breathtaking.

◆ Leap before you look. Branson is not a great believer in market research, preferring to trust his instinctive feel for what consumers want, often based on his own conversations with them.

◆ Streamline decision making. Timing is all important to Branson's success. He is a master of the decisive moment – the all-important moment when an opportunity presents itself.

◆ Get plenty of help. Something Branson is especially good at is persuading others to get involved in his projects. Whether it's Virgin employees or partner organizations, Branson's enthusiasm is infectious.

◆ Don't be afraid of making mistakes – it's the only way to learn. Branson gets fired up by new ideas and converts them into business opportunities with head-spinning speed. The downside for Virgin employees is that their illustrious leader is constantly switching from one hobby horse to the next.

NOTES

1   *Inc.* magazine, November 1987.
2   Brown, Mick, *Richard Branson: The Authorized Biography*, 4th edn, Headline, London, 1998.

Nine

SIZE DOES MATTER

"Every time a business gets too big, we start a new one. Keeping things small means keeping things personal."
– Richard Branson

While much of the corporate world seems obsessed by the size of each others organ(ization)s, Branson prefers to keep it small. The Virgin Group is effective because it maximizes the entrepreneurial spirit of its staff whilst minimizing the bureaucracy of its systems. Virgin is not a traditional hierarchical company. Rather, it is a cluster of loosely associated businesses, with their own offices and their own management teams.

Branson explains: "Every time a business gets too big, we start a new one. Keeping things small means keeping things personal; keeping things personal means keeping the people that really matter."

If you tried to design a corporate structure to provide the greatest number of employees in direct contact with their marketplace, the result would be very similar to the Virgin model. Once again, Branson instinctively does what business school professors have spent years figuring out.[1]

FROM ACORNS

Branson is a builder not a buyer, something that marks him out as a special kind of business leader. Where other business tycoons have created empires by gobbling up smaller empires, Branson has grown his own.[2] "We don't invest in land or expand by buying other large companies," he says. "Setting up companies is my skill."

In recent years, Virgin has also proved highly adept at creating joint ventures and other partnerships. This has enabled Branson to take the Virgin brand into complex marketplaces – providing the distinctive Virgin offering without having to create an organization from scratch. A good example is the 50:50 joint venture with Norwich Union, one of the UK's leading financial services companies (subsequently replaced by Australian Mutual Provident).[3] The partnership enabled Virgin to offer financial products including complex pension plans and investment packages without having to bring in all the necessary expertise in-house.

Such is the pulling power of the Virgin name that companies are only too pleased to work with Virgin. In recent years, Branson has stated that the ability to create and manage effective joint ventures is one of Virgin's core competencies.

Much of his time is spent looking at potential new businesses. A human dynamo at the centre of the Virgin empire, he is constantly sparking off new projects, which either take root and grow or simply wither on the vine. (Branson and his two-man business development team review about 50 business proposals a week. At any one time they have about four new prospects under review.)[4]

Once a promising venture has been identified, Virgin is exceptionally good at getting a business off the ground quickly – often in just a few months. Although Branson himself has the good sense both to surround himself with able people and to let people run with the ball, his own enthusiasm for the adventure invariably gets the better of him. For sheer promotional muscle, too, there is nothing quite like a Branson PR event to launch a new Virgin business.

Branson himself admits his great love and main occupation is setting up new firms. "I immerse myself in them for three months, then back off," he says. "After that I have to say to them they can only have me once or twice a year. If anything that knack for delegation is the company's core competence."[5] (Another core competence.)

The exception to the rule is Virgin Atlantic Airways, which commands the lion's share of Branson's attention. Since the sale of Virgin Music Group to Thorn EMI in 1992, it has been the jewel in the Virgin crown.

THE SIMPLE LIFE

Branson's constant quest for new businesses means that the Virgin Group is an intricate and constantly evolving web of start-ups, joint ventures and partnerships. Like an over-fertile garden, such a complex and organic empire could easily become overgrown, but Branson's promiscuous attitude to commerce is matched by his disdain for hubris. An important part of the Branson business philosophy is keep it simple – a value that he personifies.

Branson's life is remarkably uncluttered. His style is low-key and low-tech. He neither types nor uses a computer, and he didn't acquire his first mobile phone until 1993. If there is one adage that epitomizes the Branson approach it is "keep it simple."

"Branson works as if he's running a startup" observed *Forbes* magazine. "… There are no flowcharts, no traditional management hierarchies. He doesn't even know how to turn

> **"Branson works as if he's running a startup."**

on a ThinkPad, and associates Lotus not with Notes but with a very fast car ... An anachronism in the world of international business magnates, Branson keeps his appointments in a diary and scribbles ideas on his hand. It works, apparently."[6]

He carries about his person an A4 note pad bought from a stationery store. In it he scribbles his own ideas and notes on conversations and lists of tasks to do. (Such is the esteem in which he's held, that other Virgin staff imitate him by scribbling in notebooks.)

This principle applies in his private life just as much as his business life. Even his taste in food and drink is simple. A cruel remark by one business acquaintance invited to dinner with Branson described the food as "like school dinners."

Necker Island, part of the British Virgin Islands, now officially belongs to the company. It boasts a fine kitchen and wine cellar, but these are more for the benefit of visitors and Virgin executives. Branson himself shows little interest in such matters. He is said to have been scandalized when Virgin executives wanted to spend company money tasting vintage wines in restaurants, and used to have a rule never to spend more than £15 on a bottle.

Branson seems curiously detached from the material details of his life. Joan, his wife, is known to despise affectation.

Despite his huge personal wealth, Branson dresses like someone of much more modest means. Indeed, of his dress sense, it has been observed that he looks as though he picked the clothes he is wearing out of the cupboard at random in the dark – and he specializes in wearing scuffed brown shoes that look like they were on special offer in Woolworths. To Branson, none of this is important.

THE ATOMIZED EMPIRE

Much the same principle applies to the way he organizes his business empire. To avoid bureaucracy, the whole of Virgin is divided into manageable chunks. To maximize the entrepreneurial energy, and to counterbalance the risk of losses in one part of the empire infecting the other parts, each Virgin venture is intended to be a stand-alone business (even though in practice, cash generated by one business is often used to finance another). This is reflected in the structure of the Group.

Branson rejects Western corporate orthodoxy, preferring a loose grouping of companies more akin to the Japanese *keiretsu* model or family of companies: the Virgin Group is a collection of semi-independent, loosely connected empires.[7]

"The Group," he says, "is defined by its constituent parts." Each one of which is housed in a different building and encouraged to have the characteristics of a small business in its own right.

Virgin has an exceptionally decentralized structure. The Virgin brand is controlled by licensing agreements with each business. (Branson's interests are protected by ensuring that he almost invariably has an ownership stake of 50 percent or greater.) The businesses are run as independent companies by their own boards of directors.

The Virgin Group consists of a number of divisions or "clusters" of related concerns. For example, a travel cluster contains two airlines, an aviation services business and a travel company. A trading cluster includes Virgin branded vodka and cola. An entertainments cluster includes cinemas, music "Megastores," a record label and film interests. The financial services cluster sells pensions and investment plans.

**Branson on the atomized Virgin empire:
"Where we see an opportunity or gap, we start a new division. Every time a business gets too big, we start another one."**

"Where we see an opportunity or gap, we start a new division. Every time a business gets too big, we start another one," Branson says. This in turn fosters a cozy, informal atmosphere. A general rule of thumb here is that once a business gets too big to know everyone by their first name, then it is time to break it up. "Usually there are no more than 60 people in any one building," Branson says.

THE HOUSEBOAT HQ

Long before they fell out of favor with management gurus, Branson spurned the very idea of a large corporate headquarters. For many years, he ran the Virgin empire from a houseboat on the River Thames: board meetings were held around

Branson's kitchen table, or in a nearby pub. When the houseboat sank, taking most of his belongings with it, he had to make alternative arrangements.

But even then he wasn't prepared to move into conventional office space. The Virgin HQ moved upmarket with the purchase of first one, and eventually a whole string of houses, in London's trendy Holland Park. Different Virgin businesses were located in the different houses, providing each with a sense of identity, and enabling the different management teams to run their own show. For a while, Branson ran the business from an office in one of the houses which doubled as his home. He now has an office at a separate Holland Park address down the road from his house.

A visiting reporter described the Virgin hub: "The house is certainly grand (creamy walls, white molded ceilings, and all the vast stucco proportions the rich in west London acquire) but it is nothing like a modern corporate headquarters."[8]

Even today, the idea of housing the company in a tower block would be anathema to the Branson philosophy. The various Virgin businesses still operate from buildings scattered around Holland Park.[9]

GOOD IDEAS ALWAYS WELCOME

The Not Invented Here syndrome is the scourge of many business organizations, but the Virgin culture is open to new ideas from any quarter. Richard Branson has made it company policy to listen. He has also made it public knowledge that the company will take a look at business proposals from would-be partners. In reality, Virgin ends up rejecting about 95 percent out of hand, preferring to explore the ones that have serious backing.

Within the Virgin organization, Branson heads up a team of three (including himself, and an experienced venture capital expert) that meets to discuss these proposals.

He has always encouraged Virgin employees to make suggestions for improving the business – and estimates that he receives between 30 and 40 letters a day from Virgin staff. He tries to reply to their letters first. But the whole structure of the company is designed to encourage entrepreneurial behavior, and to engender a sense of belonging.

> "Out of the apparent random chaos of the Virgin organization, a business philosophy – almost an entrepreneurial blueprint – could be discerned."

As Branson's biographer Mick Brown observes: "Out of the apparent random chaos of the Virgin organization, a business philosophy – almost an entrepreneurial blueprint – could be discerned. By situating each company on its own – albeit small and determinedly unglamorous premises – overheads were kept to a minimum, but, more important, a familial atmosphere was created among staff."

SIZE DOES MATTER

The Virgin Group is effective because it maximizes the entrepreneurial spirit of its staff whilst minimizing the bureaucracy of its systems. Virgin is not a traditional hierarchical company. Rather, it is a cluster of loosely associated businesses, with their own offices and their own management teams. The Branson approach to corporate structure has five key points:

◆ Grow your own. Branson is a builder not a buyer, something that marks him out as a special kind of business leader. Where other business tycoons have created empires by gobbling up smaller empires, Branson has grown his own.
◆ Keep it simple. Branson's life is remarkably uncluttered. This adage epitomizes the Branson approach.
◆ Break it up into management molecules. To maximize the entrepreneurial energy, and to counterbalance the risk of losses in one part of the empire infecting the other parts, each Virgin venture is intended to be a stand-alone business.
◆ Keep headquarters to a minimum. Long before they fell out of favour with management gurus, Branson spurned the very idea of a large corporate headquarters.
◆ Ensure the sum of the parts is greater than the whole. Richard Branson has made it company policy to listen. He has also made it public knowledge that the company will take a look at business proposals from would-be partners.

NOTES

1   The management guru Tom Peters, in particular, has raved about the efforts of companies such as the ABB, the Swedish-Swiss engineering company, to break themselves down into small entrepreneurial units.

2   He did have an attack of takeover mania in the mid-1980s, but it was short lived. Virgin's hostile bid for EMI was cut short by the stock market crash of 1987.

3   AMP subsequently bought out Norwich Union's share in the venture.

4   Campbell, Andrew and Sadtler, David, "Corporate Breakups," *Strategy & Business*, Third Quarter 1998.

5   Rodgers, Paul, "The Branson Phenomenon," *Enterprise* magazine, March/April 1997.

6   "Richard Branson: the interview," *Forbes*, February 24, 1997.

7   Mitchell, Alan, *Leadership by Richard Branson*, Amrop International, 1995.

8   "Has he won the lottery?" *The Independent*, December 17, 1995.

9   Campbell, Andrew and Sadtler, David, "Corporate Breakups," *Strategy & Business*, Third Quarter 1998.

Ten

NEVER LOSE THE COMMON TOUCH

"There's this approachability about him, not like a pop star or other businessmen."
– Mick Brown, Branson's biographer

Richard Branson's ultimate gift is the common touch. He makes us feel as if he is one of us. In many ways this is the most difficult lesson of all. Those who want to follow in Richard Branson's footsteps have to master this skill or all the other lessons will come to nothing. More than just humility, Branson's ability to mix with people of all walks of life sets him apart from just about every other business executive you will meet. It is the key to his enduring success – and popularity.

Those who know him well say that Branson always sees things from the consumer's point of view. That's easy enough to do when you're first starting out. But to be still doing it 30 years on when you're a multi-millionaire and chairman of a group of companies worth £billions is deeply impressive. And make no mistake about it, Branson is very much in touch. How does he do it?

"I'm lucky," he says (luck is a word he uses a lot). "I can talk to people. When I first came to London as a teenager, it was such a lonely place to be. Now people come up to me in the streets or on the underground. I am lucky to know everybody."[1]

HI, I'M THE CHAIRMAN

Whenever he flies on his airline, which is about once a week, Branson takes time out to talk to the other passengers. He has been known to ham it up, donning a stewardess uniform and lipstick to serve drinks to the passengers and crew. But on many other occasions he simply makes the effort to chat with his customers and ask them what they think of his company. It is deceptively powerful.

Imagine that you are a passenger flying economy class with your family on a transatlantic flight with a leading airline. Some time into the flight, a man you immediately recognize as the airline's chairman introduces himself and politely asks if he can join you. He then proceeds to perform a few conjuring tricks to amuse the kids before producing a note pad and pencil. "What do you think of the airline?" He asks, noting any suggestions you might have. "Is there anything I can do to improve the service?"

How many airline managers – let alone chairmen and owners – take the time to talk to their customers like this? Yet, we all know that they must travel on their own flights frequently, just as Branson does. The difference is that he uses the opportunity to listen to his customers while they are far too important to talk to mere economy passengers (the flight crew of one famous airline unofficially refers to the economy class as the pig pen).

When he first set up Virgin Atlantic, Branson's policy of personally phoning 50 customers a month to ask them about the service won him adulation. Not only was he offering better service and lower fares, he managed to include the personal touch. As one observer noted: "This was in stark contrast to the monopolist monolith British Airways – which at that time was definitely not the world's favourite airline."[2]

Even if you want to be cynical about it and say he's only doing it for effect, it is very hard not to be impressed when the chairman of a major company takes the trouble to ask your views on his airline.

So, there you have it: the difference between Richard Branson and 99.9 percent of the people who run large businesses is that he treats people decently and listens to what they think. Sadly, that is enough to put him head and shoulders above most of the competition.

EVERYMAN

There is about Branson something of the Everyman figure. For no readily apparent reason, people seem to identify with him, believing he is like them. You will even hear people in Britain say that he's the original "barrow boy come good," even though his origins are many miles from London's East End. Despite his public schoolboy background, his posh accent, his expensive houses around the world, and his immense wealth and power, for some odd reason ordinary people accept him as one of their own. (Princess Diana had a similar knack of making people feel she was one of us instead of one of them.) The thing is, the man is likeable.

People who know the Bransons well say that his wife Joan keeps his feet firmly on the ground. It is his lack of front that has enabled Branson to court a popular appeal that transcends class barriers as well as national barriers.

"He doesn't do it deliberately," says Mick Brown, Branson's official biographer, "but it's a fact that his persona conceals his origins. People see him as egalitarian, déclassé, meritocratic; that, combined with his business success and his buccaneering image, makes him very attractive. And there's this approachability about him, not like a pop star or other businessmen."

Mick Brown on Branson's persona: "He doesn't do it deliberately, but it's a fact that his persona conceals his origins."

A survey[3] in May 1993, shortly after the settlement with BA, showed that Branson was the role model most young people in Britain would most like to emulate. He had been elevated almost to the status of a national hero. The psychologist who analyzed the findings noted: "There's an F Factor to Branson: he's got fame, fortune and fun." The combination makes people feel good.

People also see themselves in him. His achievements are somehow their achievements, and they love him for it. We see him doing the things we would like to do. As one interviewer observed: "This is how we think of Richard Branson: in special moments. Richard spraying champagne, like a student coming out of finals; Richard offering to run the lottery without profit, like Robin Hood; Richard defeating the great might of British Airways with all its dirty tricks, a David against a bully Goliath; Richard in goggles, a modern-day Biggles; Richard cutting a ribbon; hugging a model; hugging a Princess; hugging Scary Spice. Richard dressing up as a woman; as a bunny rabbit, as a clown."[4]

LITTLE THINGS THAT MATTER

A student who spent some time working at a company providing hot air balloon trips in the Swiss Alps remembers meeting Richard Branson. Branson was there with the aviator Per Lindstrand preparing for one of their attempts at circumnavigating the globe in a balloon. It was early in the morning and the temperature was many degrees below freezing. The student, who was preparing the balloon for a flight was frozen to the bone. As the two pilots approached he recognized Branson from his pictures on television and in newspapers.

Without thinking he slipped off his glove to shake the Virgin chairman's hand, immediately regretting it because of the gnawing cold. Branson, seeing what the young man had done, removed his own glove before shaking hands. He didn't have to. As the chairman of a large and powerful business empire, the young man meant nothing to him, and he would probably never see him again. Until that moment, however, the student was no fan of Richard Branson. In his eyes, he was just another fat cat, who preferred a jumper to a suit. But what he remembers about him is that he greeted him as an equal.

There were no cameras there to record the moment. That in itself is revealing in a way that interviews with journalists can never be. The story says a lot about Branson. It suggests that he is basically quite a nice man; that he isn't pompous or puffed up on his own self importance. It also indicates something about his style. Branson knows that the little things matter. It is a feature of all the Virgin products and services.

> Branson knows that the little things matter. It is a feature of all the Virgin products and services.

THE PEOPLE'S CHAMPION

What Branson has that others – businessmen, politicians and TV producers in particular – can only dream of is his finger on the pulse of the nation. He seems to speak for a large part of the population. Even though he himself could afford the red carpet treatment on Concorde whenever he liked, he sensed that people were fed up with the attitude of the big airlines. He was right – just as well, really, since Virgin Atlantic nearly bankrupted him. Somehow, despite the fact that his own £millions are controlled by tax-efficient offshore trusts, he correctly surmised that people with a little bit of money saved were tired of the sales patter and high charges from UK financial services companies. Somehow he knew they were ready to trust Virgin with their hard-earned cash.

Cynics will answer that he has advisers to tell him these things. But why should those advisers know any more about what annoys consumers than the people who advise the executives in any other company? In the end, even allowing for good advice, it's hard to avoid the conclusion that Branson has his own barometer of public opinion that informs his decisions.

Naturally enough, he says that he talks to people and listens to their opinions and ideas. He would say that, of course. But you don't have to be a genius to see that if you spend as much time as he does with customers, some of it has to rub off on you. Those who like to knock Richard Branson, or question his sincerity, might consider this: even if it were all a big sham, designed to make him look good, it would still mean he spent more time talking to customers than just about any other company chairman. That in itself, makes him the people's champion.

KARMA CHAMELEON

The Branson phenomenon is probably unique. It is an unusual cocktail of personality cult and business instincts. It is also curiously palatable. Perhaps the appeal of Branson is that he is different things to different people. Whether you prefer to think of him as the hippy idealist on a mission to clean up business, a lovable pirate rogue, a corporate Peter Pan, or even a robber Baron in disguise, depends on your point of view. What is undeniable is that he has dazzled the British business scene for more than two decades in a way that no other entrepreneur ever has before, or is likely to again.

> Perhaps the appeal of Branson is that he is different things to different people.

True, Branson has been fortunate to live in exciting times. From the social revolution of the 1960s through the boom of the 1980s and into the more caring 1990s, he has been there with his Virgin brand to offer an alternative take on whatever the suits were trying to sell us. He has made a large fortune doing it. But in these fat cat days when unknown faceless bureaucrats are shamelessly awarding each other huge sums of money for corporate blandness, Branson is good value.

In the end, though, it is impossible to pin down Richard Branson. He is, in the words of Boy George, one of Virgin's famous discoveries, the ultimate Karma Chameleon.

NEVER LOSE THE COMMON TOUCH

Richard Branson's ultimate gift is the common touch. He makes us feel as if he is one of us. More than just humility, Branson's ability to mix with people of all walks of life sets him apart from just about every other business executive you will meet. It is the real secret to his enduring success – and popularity. Here are the Branson lessons:

◆ Listen to people – it's the least practised management skill of them all. The difference between Richard Branson and 99.9 percent of the people who run large businesses is that he treats people decently and listens to what they think.

◆ Don't let success go to your head – a sense of humor helps, so does being thrown into swimming pools by your staff on a regular basis. There is about Branson something of the Everyman figure. For no readily apparent reason, people seem to identify with him, believing he is like them.

◆ Use your customers as consultants – they know their requirements better than the McKinseys and Bains of this world. Branson knows that the little things matter. It is a feature of all the Virgin products and services.

◆ Treat everyone as an equal; Branson is more likely to be rude to the CEO of a multinational than a check-in clerk. What Branson has that others – businessmen, politicians and TV producers in particular – can only dream of is his finger on the pulse of the nation. He seems to speak for a large part of the population.

◆ Be what people want you to be, and don't let them down. Perhaps the appeal of Branson is that he is different things to different people. What is undeniable is that he has dazzled the British business scene for more than two decades in a way that no other entrepreneur ever has before.

NOTES

1   Gerrard, Nicci, "Why do we love Richard Branson?" *The Observer*, February 8, 1998.
2   Mitchell, Alan, *Leadership by Richard Branson*, AMROP International, 1995.
3   Sponsored by the TSB.
4   Gerrard, Nicci, "Why do we love Richard Branson," *The Observer*, February 8, 1998.

HOW TO BUILD A BRAND THE BRANSON WAY

Business visionary or personality cult? Richard Branson's Virgin brand is unique. No other company has ever created anything quite like it. Only time will tell whether Branson has invented a new blueprint for capitalism for the 21st Century, or is simply a better sales man. Nirvana or more of the same with a different spin? It all depends on your point of view.

For those who want to follow in his footsteps, here are the secrets of his success.

1 Pick on someone bigger than you: attack dominant market players

Richard Branson has made a career out of playing David to the other guy's Goliath. Where some entrepreneurs might take one look at the market dominance of the big players and think better of it, Branson actually delights in taking on and outmaneuvering large corporations.

The Branson strategy is:

◆ make business a crusade

◆ hoist a pirate flag

◆ play the underdog

◆ pick your battles

◆ hit them where it hurts.

2 Do the hippy, hippy shake

Branson's affinity with flower power and the whole 1960s move-ment is less a commitment to a set of principles or political beliefs, and much more related to being in tune with the times – one of his greatest business attributes. Branson's alternative management style offers the following lessons to aspiring mo-guls, including:

◆ don't be a bread head

◆ dress down every day (not just Fridays)

◆ put people first

◆ blur the divide between work and play

◆ shake it up (don't imitate, innovate).

3 Haggle: everything's negotiable

One of Richard Branson's less appreciated talents is a razor sharp negotiating technique. Nice guys finish last, or so they say, but not Branson. Despite – or perhaps because of – his Mr Nice Guy image, Branson rarely comes out second best in any of the deals he makes. Charisma and considerable personal charm belie a calculating business brain.

The lessons from the Branson school of negotiating are:

◆ nice guys finish first

◆ never say never

◆ talk softly and carry a big stick

◆ act on good advice

◆ cover the upside as well as the downside.

4 Make work fun

Business, in Richard Branson's view, should be fun. Creating an exciting work culture is the best way to motivate and retain good people; it also means you don't have to pay them as much.

Unlike the computer whiz-kids Bill Gates and Steve Jobs, Branson has never invented any product of a revolutionary nature. All the industries he has succeeded in are conventional ones with little in common except that they are mature and dominated by large players. So what is it that Richard Branson knows about business that other people who have been in these conventional industries for years have failed to grasp?

The answer is simple. Branson has the ability to motivate people and push them to the limit. He possesses a remarkable ability to inspire others to achieve what they didn't know they were capable of. The Branson technique for managing people provides the following lessons:

◆ it pays to play

◆ let employees loose

◆ encourage informality – stay on first name terms

◆ praise people rather than criticizing them

◆ make business an adventure.

5 Do right by your brand

One of the most frequently asked questions about Virgin is how far the brand can stretch. Some commentators believe that, by putting the Virgin name on such a wide range of products and services, Branson risks seriously diluting the brand. His answer to this criticism is that as long as the brand's integrity is not compromised, then it is infinitely elastic.

Lessons from Branson, the brand master are:

◆ a good brand travels

brand elasticity is infinite

love honor and cherish your brand

◆ rules are for breaking

be cheeky.

Virgin's five brand values are:

value for money

quality

fun/cheek

innovation

challenge.

6 Smile for the cameras

Richard Branson has turned himself into a walking, talking logo. Where McDonald's has Ronald McDonald, a six foot, ginger-haired clown, and Disney has Mickey Mouse; Virgin has its goofy chairman. Every time his picture appears in a newspaper or magazine, it promotes the Virgin brand.

This is entirely deliberate, and probably one of the most effective promotional strategies ever employed by a company. The risk to the reputation of the brand, of course, is correspondingly high should Branson's personal image become tarnished.

To date, however, it has proved highly successful, enabling him to build the Virgin brand on a shoestring advertising budget.

◆ Understand what the media want, and give it to them

◆ think in pictures

◆ stand up and be counted

◆ remember, philanthropy and stamp collecting are two different things

◆ know when to duck.

7 Don't lead sheep, herd cats

Liberate creativity, and encourage people to do what they do best.

◆ Be a back-seat leader

◆ act as a catalyst

◆ surround yourself with talented people

◆ encourage chaos

◆ make good ideas welcome (wherever they come from).

8 Move faster than a speeding bullet

Branson moves quickly when an opportunity presents itself.

◆ Seize the moment (beware of paralysis by analysis)

◆ leap before you look (avoid paralysis by analysis)

◆ streamline decision making

◆ use joint ventures to leverage expertise

◆ make plenty of mistakes (it's the only way to learn).

9 Size does matter

If you're a Virgin, then size is important to you. The Virgin Group is effective because it maximizes the entrepreneurial spirit of its staff whilst minimizing the bureaucracy of its systems. Virgin is not a traditional hierarchical company. Rather, it is a cluster of loosely associated businesses, with their own offices and their own management teams.

If you tried to design a corporate structure to provide the greatest number of employees in direct contact with their marketplace, the result would be very similar to the Virgin model. Once again, Branson instinctively does what business school professors spend years figuring out. The essence of the Branson approach to corporate structure has five key points:

- ◆ grow your own

- ◆ keep it simple

- ◆ break up your empire into small molecules

- ◆ keep headquarters to a minimum

- ◆ put out the welcome mat for good ideas.

10   Never lose the common touch

In many ways this is the most difficult lesson of all. Those who want to follow in Richard Branson's footsteps have to master this or all the other lessons will come to nothing. More than just humility, Branson's ability to mix with people of all walks of life sets him apart from just about every other business executive you will meet. It is the real secret to his enduring success – and popularity.

- ◆ Listen to people – customers and employees are a good place to start

- ◆ don't let success go to your head

- ◆ use your customers as consultants – they know their requirements better than the McKinseys and Bains of this world

- ◆ treat everyone as an equal; one of Branson's most endearing traits is that he is more likely to be rude to the CEO of a multinational than a check-in clerk

- ◆ be what people want you to be – be a chameleon.

LAST WORD

In his book *Virgin King*, Tim Jackson observes that Branson's motto should be *ars est celare artem* – the art lies in concealing the art. Branson's business rivals have paid dearly for underestimating him; for mistaking his public persona for the whole story. There is much more to the Virgin chairman than his publicity stunts and schoolboy pranks – ask Lord King.

But perhaps the real secret of Branson is that he is different things to different people. Whether you prefer to think of him as the hippy idealist on a mission to clean up business, a lovable pirate rogue, a corporate Peter Pan, or even a robber baron in disguise, depends on your point of view. What is undeniable is that he has dominated the British business scene for more than two decades in a way that no other entrepreneur ever has before, or is likely to again.

Branson has been fortunate to live in exciting times. From the social revolution of the 1960s through the halcyon days of the 1980s, into the more caring 1990s, and on to the new millennium he has been there with his Virgin brand to offer an alternative take on whatever the suits were trying to sell us. You can't help thinking though that he would have made any time interesting.

In the end, though, it is impossible to put Richard Branson in a specimen jar. He is, in the words of Boy George, one of Virgin's most famous discoveries, the ultimate Karma Chameleon, changing color to suit his surroundings. He has brought his many colors to the world of consumers, employees and big business. So far, at least, he has given the suits a damn good run for their money.

INDEX